The
Biblical Basis
for the *Eucharist*

D1565225

The
Biblical Basis
for the *Eucharist*

JOHN SALZA

Our Sunday Visitor Publishing Division
Our Sunday Visitor, Inc.
Huntington, Indiana 46750

Nihil Obstat: Rev. Michael Heintz
Censor Librorum
Imprimatur: ✠ John M. D'Arcy
Bishop of Fort Wayne-South Bend
February 17, 2008

Our Sunday Visitor Publishing Division
Our Sunday Visitor, Inc.
200 Noll Plaza
Huntington, IN 46750

ISBN: 978-1-59276-336-8 (Inventory No. T435)
LCCN: 2008923965

Cover design by Amanda Miller
Cover image: Design Pics
Interior design by Sherri L. Hoffman

PRINTED IN THE UNITED STATES OF AMERICA

To my dear brother and friend,

FR. PAUL A. GRIZZELLE-REID, S.C.J.

Thank you for your love and priestly devotion
to the Most Holy Eucharist.

Contents

Preface

Throughout the world, for 2,000 years, the Catholic Church has been celebrating the Eucharist as the source and summit of the Christian faith. Jesus Christ instituted the Eucharist[1] at the Last Supper, the night before He died, which formally inaugurated the implementation of the New Covenant. In the presence of His apostles, Jesus took bread, gave thanks, and said, "This is my body;" He also took a cup of wine, and said, "This is the cup of my blood." He then commanded His apostles to "do this in memory of me."[2]

The doctrine of the Eucharist is one of the most divisive doctrines separating Catholics and Protestants. This is because the doctrine of the Eucharist is as incredible and scandalous as the doctrine of the Incarnation itself. The Catholic Church teaches that whenever a priest celebrates the Holy Mass,[3] God changes the bread and wine offered by the priest into the Body and Blood of Jesus Christ. The Church calls this miraculous change in the substance of the bread and wine *transubstantiation* (meaning "change in substance").

Because the priest consecrates the bread and wine separately, as Jesus did at the Last Supper, Christ is made present in an

---

[1] The word "Eucharist" comes from the Greek word *eucharistein*, which means "thanksgiving."

[2] Mt 26:26-28; Mk 14:22-24; Lk 22:19-20; 1 Cor 11:23-25.

[3] The word "Mass" comes from the Latin *missio*, which refers to a "dismissal, or being projected forth like a projectile, and hence the word missile." The Church adopted the term to emphasize that the Eucharistic life is lived principally in the world after the congregants have been "dismissed" from the celebration. In the Traditional Latin Mass, the priest concludes the celebration by saying: *Ite missa est* (Go, it [the assembly] has been sent).

immolated state on the altar. As the species of the transubstantiated bread and wine signify the actual separation of Christ's Body and Blood during His Passion, Christ is offered to God in sacrifice.[4] This offering *reenacts* the very sacrifice that Jesus offered on the Cross two thousand years ago. It is *not* a new or different sacrifice; it is the *same* sacrifice of Calvary, re-presented sacramentally in an unbloody manner. Following the sacrificial offering, Catholics receive the Body and Blood of Christ under the appearance of bread and wine in Holy Communion

It should be no surprise that many believers in Jesus Christ reject this teaching. Even many that Jesus taught face-to-face found this doctrine too difficult to accept. When Jesus said, "Unless you eat the flesh of the Son of Man and drink his blood, you have no life in you,"[5] many chose to abandon Him (Jn 6:66). Jesus then turned to His twelve apostles and asked, "Will you also go away?" (Jn 6:67). Jesus asks our non-Catholic Christian friends the same question.

Philosophically speaking, it can be much easier to accept the doctrine of the Eucharist than the doctrine of the Incarnation. It takes a greater leap of faith to believe that the almighty and incomprehensible God would become a little, helpless infant. In fact, the perceived implausibility of the Incarnation is the main reason why people do not become Christians. However, the majority of the people who become Christians also believe in the Eucharist.[6] This makes sense. As my seven-year-old daughter explained to me, if we can believe that God could create every-

---

[4] This "signification" does not suggest that Christ's Body and Blood are literally separated on the altar, for when we receive the consecrated host or the consecrated wine, we receive the whole Christ —Body, Blood, Soul, and Divinity.

[5] Jn 6:54.

[6] Similar to Catholics and the Orthodox, some Anglican and Lutheran churches also believe in a real presence of Christ in the Eucharist (although the Anglican and Lutheran churches do not have a valid priesthood and hence the sacrament is not confected).

thing out of nothing (i.e., the universe), then it is easy to believe that *He can change something into something else* (i.e., bread and wine into Christ's Body and Blood).

Non-Catholic Christians object to the Eucharist as a sacrifice because the book of Hebrews says that Jesus offered His sacrifice "once for all."[7] On that basis, Protestants conclude that the Mass makes the Cross of Calvary insufficient to save us, and adds to the "finished work of Christ." At first blush, these passages which describe Christ's sacrifice as "once for all" make the Protestant objection seem plausible.

However, as we will examine in detail, the "once for all" dimension of Jesus' sacrifice means the sacrifice is *perpetual*, not completed in a moment in time. This is why the same book of Hebrews uses "once for all" to describe both Jesus' *appearance* in heaven[8] as well as His *sacrifice*[9] — two realities that the Scriptures inextricably link together. Just as Jesus appeared in heaven once for all, and His appearance is ongoing, Jesus offered His sacrifice once for all, and the sacrifice is ongoing. In the context of Jesus' perpetual appearance in heaven, the Scriptures also teach that Jesus *intercedes* for us before the Father for the purpose of *saving* us.[10]

We might first ask our Protestant friends why Jesus needs to intercede for us to save us if His work on the Cross was "finished" and we need only to accept His work by faith alone. We might also ask why the requirement to have faith in Jesus' sacrifice is not "adding" to the work of the Cross, and why the Bible repeatedly warns true believers that they will be condemned if they don't persevere in that faith.[11]

---

[7] See Heb 7:27; 9:12, 26;10:10-14.

[8] Heb 9:12, 26.

[9] Heb 7:27.

[10] Heb 7:25; 9:24; Rom 8:34.

[11] For example, over one-half of the book of Hebrews is devoted to warning believing Christians about falling away from the faith (e.g., Heb 3:1, 6, 12-14; 4:1, 11-14; 6:4-6, 11-12; 10:26-17, 35-38; 12:1-3, 14-17, 25, 29).

The Scriptures teach that Jesus appears in heaven as our Intercessor to present His priestly sacrifice to the Father *so that the Father will forgive our sins and give us the graces necessary for salvation.* While Jesus' suffering and death is completed, His once-for-all sacrifice has an eternal dimension which transcends time and space. This is why Jesus' suffering and death is always described in the past tense, but His sacrifice is never so described.[12]

When Jesus commanded His apostles to "do this" in His memory, He established the New Testament priesthood, so that the sacrifice which He presents as High Priest to the Father in heaven would also be sacramentally offered by His priests on earth (who really are acting in the one person of the one priest, Jesus Christ). In this way, its saving power would be applied to people in every generation and location throughout the ages. God's moment-by-moment application of the Cross to sinners is necessary because we sin moment-by-moment, and God deals with us within the temporal realm in which He created us.

Therefore, the Mass is not about *adding* to the sacrifice of Christ; it is about *applying* the sacrifice to each person throughout time and space so that each of us can receive what the Lord has won for us — namely, forgiveness of sin and the grace to be saved. Protestants certainly relate to this idea, for they believe the merits of the Cross are applied *only* to those who have faith in Jesus (while also believing that faith doesn't "add" to the work of the Cross). Thus, the application of the Cross to sinners is also a part of Protestant theology. The difference is *how* the merits of the Cross are applied.[13]

---

[12] Heb 2:18; 5:7-8.

[13] This difference regards both when Christ's sacrifice is applied (one-time event vis-à-vis moment-by-moment basis) and what criteria God uses to appropriate its merits to sinners (by faith alone vis-à-vis faith accompanied by baptism, hope, love, good works, repentance, obedience, confession, perseverance, etc.).

Because the Mass re-presents the sacrifice of the Cross, the Church teaches that the sacrifice of the Mass is truly *propitiatory*.[14] That is, when God sees the sacrifice of the Mass, He is "propitiated" or appeased, and responds by dispensing His grace, mercy, and forgiveness for the many sins that we daily commit. I would even say that the celebration of the Mass is the very reason why God doesn't come immediately to condemn the world for its many and grievous sins. We could survive more easily without food and water than the sacrifice of the Mass.

This raises some fundamental questions about God that bear upon our understanding of the Mass: Why did God wish to see the sacrifice of Calvary in the first place? Why would God desire such a brutal sacrifice from His Incarnate Son? Why does God will to be appeased to forgive sin? Once we understand the answers to these questions, we will be better enabled to understand why God desires to see the re-presentation of the Cross in the Holy Mass. Then, we will understand why participating in the sacrifice of the Mass is the worship that God enjoins on all Christians.

This book explores the biblical basis for the Catholic Church's teaching on the Eucharist and the Holy Mass. The book sets forth clear, scriptural support for the Church's teaching about the propitiatory nature of Christ's sacrifice, its ongoing presentation to the Father, its application to the human race, and the Real Presence of Christ in the Eucharist. Our belief in the Eucharist goes to the very heart and soul of our Christianity — namely, our understanding of who God is and how He has chosen to save us from our sins.

The Catholic Church has taught the same thing about the Eucharist since its very beginning, twenty centuries ago. This is

---

[14] See Council of Trent, Session XXII, *Doctrine Concerning the Sacrifice of the Mass*, Chapter II and Canon 3 (September 17, 1562).

well-documented. To give the reader a broader perspective, I have also included quotes from the early Church Fathers during the first five centuries of the Church. These statements provide additional testimony in support of the Church's teaching on the Eucharist.

One of the earliest witnesses comes from Ignatius, bishop of Antioch, around A.D. 107. Ignatius learned about the Eucharist directly from the Apostle John and his protégé, Polycarp. In his letter to the Smyrnaeans, Ignatius reproves those who deny the Catholic Church's teaching on the Eucharist as he says:

> They abstain from the Eucharist and from prayer, because they do not admit that the Eucharist is the Flesh of our Savior Jesus Christ, the same Flesh which suffered for our sins and which the Father, in His graciousness, raised from the dead.

This and many other similar quotes are provided in Chapter IV.

The early Fathers were unanimous in their belief of the Eucharistic sacrifice, which they held to be the Tradition handed down to them from the apostles. For any honest Christian, it will be difficult to deny the scriptural, patristic, and historical support for the Church's teaching on the Eucharist. This is why the Eucharist is one of the main reasons that Protestant Christians come home to the Catholic Church.

I pray that Catholics who read this book develop a greater appreciation for the sacrifice of the Mass and a deeper relationship with our Eucharistic Lord. I pray also that Catholic priests are reinvigorated in their devotions to the Holy Eucharist and faithfully live out the sacrifice they offer. Finally, I pray to the Lord that non-Catholic Christians and all people discover the Catholic and Apostolic faith and finally come to know our Lord Jesus "in the breaking of the bread" (Lk 24:35).

"But God chose what is foolish in the world to shame the wise, God chose what is weak in the world to shame the strong" (1 Cor 1:27).

John Salza
Feast of St. Andrew, Apostle
November 30, 2006, *Anno Domini*

CHAPTER I

The Nature of God

GOD AND COVENANT

When Jesus instituted the Eucharistic sacrifice at the Last Supper, He said, "This is my blood of the covenant."[1] This is the only time that Jesus uses the word "covenant" in the New Testament Scriptures. Therefore, we begin our study by looking at the meaning of "covenant." The concept of covenant is foundational for understanding God, the Eucharist, and the atoning work of Christ.

The word *covenant* comes from the Latin word *convenire*, which means "to come together" or "to agree." A covenant is an agreement between two parties to adhere to certain rules for their mutual benefit. If the parties faithfully abide by the covenant, they will experience the blessings of the covenant relationship. However, if one of the parties breaches the agreement, the party will suffer the penalties stipulated in the covenant.

There are two primary factors that distinguish covenants from contracts. First, a contract is an exchange of property or services, whereas a covenant *is an exchange of persons*. In making a covenant, the parties effectively say, "I am yours, and you are mine." Thus, a covenant goes beyond a mere legal arrangement (e.g., what can and cannot be done). A covenant also includes provisions for the personal welfare of the parties, such as love,

---

[1] Mt 26:28; Mk 14:24; similar words are used in Lk 22:20 and 1 Cor 11:25.

concern, and forgiveness. While the legal provisions are necessary for the effective administration of the covenant, it is the personal dimensions of the covenant that sustain the relationship between the parties. Love is stronger than law. Since "God is love,"[2] He desires a personal relationship with us based on covenant, not contract.

Second, a contract is made by giving a *promise*; a covenant is made only by swearing an *oath*. In a contract, a person says, "I give you my word" and signs his name to the agreement. Thus, the promise is based on the person's own reputation. In a covenant, the person says, "I swear to God" and "So help me God," thereby invoking God to both witness the promise and assist in fulfilling it. In swearing the oath, the person puts himself under God's divine judgment and will trigger the penalties of the covenant if he violates his oath (e.g., "I'll be damned"). Thus, a covenant is a much stronger and graver form of commitment than a contract.

Marriage is the best example of a covenant relationship between human beings. In marriage, a man and a woman enter into a legal arrangement whereby they are governed by laws that protect their welfare and the welfare of their children. Although it is a legal arrangement, the marriage bond is not a contract but a covenant. The personal aspects of the bond supersede the legal ones because the relationship is fundamentally based upon the love that the spouses have for each other. The marriage relationship is the model for biblical covenants.[3] In fact, God considers the New Covenant as a marriage between Christ and the Church.[4] Just as marriage is a sacrament, Paul calls Christ's relationship with the Church "a great sacrament."[5] At the end of

---

[2] 1 Jn 4:8, 16.

[3] See, for example, Is 62:5; Jer 3:20; Hos 2:16; Gal 4:22-31.

[4] See Eph 5:22-33.

[5] Eph 5:32, Douay-Rheims (DR).

time, the Church will be presented to Christ "as a bride adorned for her husband" (Apoc 21:2).[6]

The Latin word for *oath*, which is the foundation of the covenant relationship, is *sacramentum* (in English, "sacrament"). The Hebrew word for "oath-swearing" is *sheba*, a term based on the word "seven." In Hebrew, to swear an oath literally means "to seven oneself."[7] In the Old Covenant, God frequently associated the number seven with the worship that He enjoined on His people, beginning with Adam and "seventh day." On the seventh day (the "Sabbath"), God required Adam and his family to renew their covenant with Him through prayer, worship, and rest (Gen 2:2-3). Scripture provides many other examples in the Old Covenant where God connects "seven" with "worship."[8]

While not obvious to most Protestants, the relationship between "seven," "sacraments," and "worship" should be self-evident to Catholics. In making the Old Covenant obsolete, Jesus Christ instituted *seven sacraments as the worship laws of the New Covenant.*[9] In these seven sacraments, God has "sevened Himself" to humanity once and for all by promising us the love, forgiveness, and graces necessary for our salvation. At the con-

---

[6] Just as a husband and wife renew their covenant with each other by becoming one flesh in the marital embrace, Catholics renew their covenant with God by becoming one flesh with Jesus Christ in the Eucharist.

[7] See, for example, Gen 21:27-32.

[8] Gen 7:2-3; 21:28-30; Ex 12:15-16, 19; 13:6-7; 16:26-27, 29-20; 20:10-11; 23:11-12, 15; 24:16; 29:30, 35, 37; 31:15, 17; 34:18, 21; 35:2; 37:23; Lev 4:6, 17; 8:11, 33, 35; 16:14, 19, 29; 22:27; 23:3, 6, 8, 15-16, 18, 24, 27, 34, 36, 39-42; 25:4, 8-9; Num 28:11, 17, 19, 21, 24-25, 27, 29; 29:1-2, 4, 7-8, 10, 12, 32, 36; Deut 5:14; 16:3-4, 8-9, 13, 15; Josh 6:4, 6, 8, 13, 15-16; Judg 6:25; 14:12, 17-18; 1 Sam 6:1; 31:13; 2 Kings 5:10, 14; 1 Chron 15:26; 2 Chron 7:8-10; 13:9; 15:11; 17:11; 29:21; 30:21-24; Ezek 6:22; Neh 8:2, 14, 18; Job 42:8; Ps 12:6; 119:164; Ezek 3:15-16; 30:20; 45:20-21, 23, 25; Zech 3:9; 4:10; 7:5; 8:19.

[9] The seven sacraments are: Baptism, Penance, the Eucharist, Confirmation, Holy Matrimony, Holy Orders, and Extreme Unction.

summation of the New Covenant, we will "worship" and "rest" with God in one eternal "Sabbath" day.

Moreover, God ratified His promise of grace with an oath (a *sacramentum*).[10] In this oath, God gave us His Eternal Word, which became flesh and dwelled among us.[11] To obtain the Father's grace and mercy, the Word bore the curses of the Old Covenant by being hung on a tree.[12]

While all seven sacraments revitalize our covenant with God, the Eucharist brings about our covenant relationship with Him *par excellence*. As we will learn, this is because we share in the flesh and blood of His only begotten Son. In this intimate, personal communion, we receive the Spirit of divine sonship and are able, with Christ, to cry, "Abba, Father."[13] As Peter says, we "become partakers of the divine nature" (1 Pet 2:4). Because the Eucharistic sacrifice re-presents Christ's death on Calvary, the salutary act that secured our redemption, the Eucharist is the foundation of the New Covenant. This is why Jesus called the Eucharist "the *new covenant* in my blood."[14]

The First Covenant

From the Biblical account of Adam and Eve, rich in imagery, we can draw deep lessons. God made His first covenant with Adam and Eve, our first parents, at the beginning of creation. God gave Himself to Adam by imprinting upon him His own divine image and likeness (Gen 1:26-27). Eve was bound to the Adamic covenant by being created from Adam's rib and shared in God's image and likeness through her covenant relationship with

---

[10] Heb 6:16-17; 7:21, 28. See also Gen 17:4-7; 22:16-18 where God promised the New Covenant of grace to Abraham and his descendants.

[11] Jn 1:1, 14.

[12] Deut 21:23; Gal 3:13.

[13] Rom 8:15; Gal 4:6.

[14] Lk 22:20.

Adam.[15] Adam and Eve, in return, were to give themselves fully to God through faithful obedience to the covenant provisions. There was to be a free and loving exchange of interpersonal communion between God and our first parents.

Like all covenants, this first covenant had both personal and legal aspects. On the personal side, Adam and Eve would enjoy God's love, protection, and sustenance in the Garden of Eden. On the legal side, Adam and Eve were required to work in the Garden and refrain from eating of the tree of the knowledge of good and evil, lest they suffer death. If Adam and Eve were faithful to the covenant, they would enjoy intimate union with God and live forever with Him.

We all know what happened in the story. Tempted by Satan, Adam and Eve disobeyed God's commandment and ate the forbidden fruit (Gen 3:1-7). Their violation of the covenant triggered its legal penalties, namely, suffering and death.[16] Because God was seemingly so offended by this sin, He subjected all men to the penal sanctions of the covenant.[17] Thus, the first covenant, originally designed to give eternal life, actually brought eternal death to all men. Paul says, "The very commandment which promised life proved to be death to me" (Rom 7:10).

The Necessity of a New Covenant

Although Adam and Eve's disobedience activated the punitive sanctions of the covenant, God continued to love Adam and

---

[15] Gen 2:21-23. Adam uses vivid, covenant language to describe his wife: "This at last is bone of my bones and flesh of my flesh" (v. 23).

[16] Gen 3:17-19; Rom 5:14; see also Hos 6:7. Although Eve was first deceived by Satan and labeled the "transgressor" (1 Tim 2:14), the Church teaches that Adam's disobedience, not Eve's, caused Original Sin. This is because God gave Adam authority over Eve as the head of his family (see Gen 2:18; 1 Tim 2:13; 1 Cor 11:9). If Adam would have obeyed God and reproved Eve for her transgression, God would have preserved the human race from sin.

[17] See Rom 5:12.

Eve and still desired to grant them and their progeny eternal life. Because of His loving nature, God would not forget about the personal dimensions of the covenant (e.g., forgiveness). Because the penalty of death had been irrevocably triggered, God would have to replace the first covenant with another covenant.

However, because God is perfectly just and holy, He could not just ignore Adam and Eve's sin. To preserve His honor while saving humanity from eternal death, God would require a satisfaction for sin.[18] God provided the answer in His only begotten Son, Jesus Christ. As we will study later on, Jesus' New Covenant sacrifice would be the perfect atonement for sin, so that man could have life again. Paul says, "For as in Adam all die, so also in Christ shall all be made alive" (1 Cor 15:22).

Because Adam and Eve violated the first covenant by their lack of faith in God, God would require *faith* as the basis for entering into the New Covenant. *All would have to pass the test that Adam and Eve failed.* While the New Covenant would also have legal provisions, God would require people to base their relationship with Him on the personal dimensions of the Covenant, not the legal ones. If people would approach God with personal *faith* in Him, then God would give them the *grace* of the New Covenant.[19] If they would approach God based on impersonal "works of law," they would remained condemned.[20]

---

[18] God was not compelled by necessity to send Christ to atone for sin. As Thomas Aquinas teaches, because God is omnipotent and perfectly free, it was possible for God to save man other than by Christ's Passion. Further, because God has no one higher than Himself, it would not have been an offense against justice for God to have willed our salvation without a satisfaction (He would have wronged no one in doing so). However, the Father's will to send Christ to die for sin was the most suitable way, demonstrating *par excellence* His mercy and love for humanity. Thus, Aquinas teaches that Christ's death was not a necessity from compulsion (because God is free) but a necessity from supposition (supposing God willed Christ's death, which He did).

[19] Rom 3:20, 22, 28; Gal 2:16; Phil 3:9; Eph 2:8-9.

[20] See Rom 3:20, 28; Gal 2:16. See also Jn 3:18.

This means that God began offering humanity the benefits of the New Covenant beginning with Adam and Eve, many centuries before the coming of Christ.[21] How? Because God, in His divine foreknowledge, knew that Christ's future sacrifice to make atonement for sin was certain to occur. Scripture says that Jesus was "delivered up according to the definite plan and foreknowledge of God."[22] Since God is outside of time and all moments are present to Him in their immediacy, the Father could see His Son's future sacrifice and apply the gracious merits of that sacrifice to those who approached Him in faith, even before it occurred.

Paul addresses this concept of faith and grace as he writes about the Old Testament saints who lived prior to the coming of Christ:

- *By faith* Abel offered to God a more acceptable sacrifice than Cain, through which he received approval as righteous."[23] Thus, "the Lord looked with grace on Abel and his offering, but on Cain and his offering he did not look with grace."[24]
- "*By faith* Noah, being warned by God concerning events as yet unseen, took heed and constructed an ark for the saving of his household . . . and became an heir of the righteousness which comes *by faith*."[25] Thus, "Noah found *grace* in the eyes of the Lord."[26]
- "*By faith* Abraham obeyed when he was called to go out to a place which he was to receive as an inheritance";[27] "*By*

---

[21] See Gen 3:15, where God promises Adam and Eve a Savior in what is called the *Protoevangelium*, or "First Gospel."

[22] Acts 2:23; see also 1 Pet 1:20.

[23] Heb 11:4; see also Gen 4:4.

[24] Gen 4:4-5, New International Version (NIV).

[25] Heb 11:7; see also Gen 6:8.

[26] Gen 6:8 (NIV).

[27] Heb 11:8.

faith Abraham, when he was tested, offered up Isaac";[28] "We say that *faith* was reckoned to Abraham as righteousness."[29]

As these Scriptures demonstrate, God began instituting the provisions of the New Covenant before the coming of Christ, by granting *grace* to those who approached Him in *faith*.[30] Because Jesus at the Last Supper instituted the Eucharist as the sign and seal of "the New Covenant in His Blood," we must have faith in the Eucharist. Paul makes this clear when he says that God purposed Christ "to be a propitiation, through *faith* in his blood" (Rom 3:25). If we have *faith* in the blood of Christ which He offers in the Eucharist, we receive the *grace* of the New Covenant. This grace makes us adopted sons and daughters of the Father and heirs of heaven.

GOD'S ANGER AT SIN AND DESIRE TO BE APPEASED

As we have just seen, God condemned to death the entire human race for the sin of Adam. To do such a thing demonstrates how much sin offends God and transgresses the order of His divine justice. After all, every single person since Adam is subject to suffering and death because of Adam's sin. To understand how Christ appeased God's anger and satisfied the demands of His strict justice, let's first look at the God whose anger is clearly related throughout the Scriptures.

God is an intensely personal being who desires an intimate relationship with human beings. When we transgress God's laws

---

[28] Heb 11:17; see also Gal 5:4.

[29] Rom 4:9.

[30] Before Christ's coming, God administered His covenant through His chosen people, Israel. With the death and resurrection of Christ, God now administers His covenant through the Church, the new Israel (Gal 6:16).

(i.e., commit sin), we injure our relationship with God by refusing to give Him the love and obedience we owe Him, and by upsetting the order of divine justice with which God governs the universe. As a personal being, Scripture reveals that God responds with "anger" when we oppose His justice and friendship through sin. Although God is sovereign and immutable, He interacts with and responds to human actions. If God were an impersonal deity, like a force of nature or a deistic "Great Architect of the Universe," our sins would elicit no response from Him.[31]

The Scriptures are full of examples of God expressing His righteous anger at sin. In the Old Testament we read:

- Then the *anger* of the LORD was kindled against Moses (Ex 4:14).
- The *anger* of the LORD blazed hotly (Num 11:10).[32]
- "That the LORD may turn from the fierceness of his *anger*" (Deut 13:17).[33]
- The *anger* of the LORD burned against the people of Israel (Josh 7:1).[34]
- They provoked the LORD to *anger* (Judg 2:12).[35]
- Again the *anger* of the LORD was kindled against Israel (2 Sam 24:1).[36]

---

[31] When we say God "responds" to sin, we don't mean to imply that God somehow changes, for God's will is immutable and cannot change (Mal 3:6; Num 23:19). Rather, we mean that God wills the sinner to change because God wills all men to be saved (1 Tim 2:4). God fulfills His will by constantly giving man grace to repent. If man repents, God forgives. If man does not repent, God punishes. God's "response" (whether it's forgiveness, punishment, or both) comes from His same immutable will to save the sinner.

[32] See also Num 11:11; 12:9; 22:22; 25:3-4; 32:13-14.

[33] See also Deut 1:34; 4:25; 6:15; 7:4; 9:18-19; 11:17; 29:20, 23-24, 27-28; 31:17, 29; 32:16, 22.

[34] See also Josh 23:16.

[35] See also Judges 2:14, 20; 3:8; 6:39; 10:7.

[36] See also 2 Sam 6:7.

- The *anger* of the LORD was kindled against his people (Is 5:25).
- And they did wicked things, provoking the LORD to *anger* (2 Kings 17:11).[37]

God's anger is also expressed in the New Testament, for example:

- You are storing up *wrath* for yourself on the day of *wrath* when God's righteous judgment will be revealed (Rom 2:5).
- Since, therefore, we are now justified by his blood, much more shall we be saved by him from the *wrath* of God (Rom 5:9).
- As I swore in my *wrath*, "They shall never enter my rest" (Heb 3:11).[38]
- He also shall drink the wine of God's *wrath*, poured unmixed into the cup of his *anger* (Apoc 14:10).

One of the more striking examples of God's anger is recorded in the book of Genesis. During the time of Noah, the world became so evil that God expressed His anger in terms of grief and regret: "And the LORD was sorry that he had made man on earth, and it *grieved* him to his heart" (Gen 6:6). As a result of His anger, God sent a global flood on the earth for forty days and nights to destroy man and beast alike.[39] However, God spared Noah and his family, for "Noah found favor in the eyes of the LORD" (Gen 6:8).

These and many other passages in Scripture reveal that God is an intensely personal being whose will is completely opposed to evil and sin. As such, He requires us to recognize His personality and goodness, respect His honor and authority, and obey

---

[37] See also 1 Kings 14:9, 15; 15:30; 16:2, 7, 13, 26, 33; 21:22; 22:53; and 2 Kings 13:3; 17:17; 21:6, 15; 22:17; 23:19; 24:20. There are many other similar examples throughout the rest of the Old Testament.

[38] See also Heb 4:3.

[39] See Gen 4:7, 11-24.

His laws of equity and justice. Because He is such a personal being, God is offended by those who sin against Him. Because Adam's sin was an infinite insult against God that brought corruption and death to humanity, God would require a sacrifice of infinite worth to counterbalance the insult.

To preserve His honor and restore the equality of His justice, God willed to be *propitiated* before He could grant mercy and forgiveness to man. *Propitiation* is the act of appeasing God by sacrifice, which averts His anger and elicits His forgiveness.[40] When someone propitiates God through sacrifice, he recognizes God's worth, respects His honor, and seeks to repair the injured relationship. In short, he demonstrates his love for God.[41]

As personal beings made in God's image and likeness, we can relate to the idea of propitiation and appeasement in our own interactions. When someone offends us, we are more willing to accept the offender back into our good graces if they repent of the offense and make some kind of sacrifice to us. The book of Proverbs says, "A gift in secret averts anger" (21:4). Further, the more holy and honorable a person is, the more an offender must to do appease him.

God can be propitiated by certain human beings because He is sensitive both to a man's sin *and* a righteous man's zeal to appease His anger against the sin. This is why God says:

> Run to and fro through the streets of Jerusalem, look and take note! Search her squares to see if you can find a man, one *who does justice and seeks truth*; that I may pardon her.
>
> — JER 5:1

---

[40] Aquinas says, "A sacrifice properly so called is something done for that honor which is properly due to God, in order to appease Him" (*Summa Theologica*, III, Q. 48, Art. 3).

[41] Our ability to appease God is itself a grace from God. God, as Prime Mover, moves people to propitiate Him by the power of His grace. Hence, as Augustine says, when God accepts our works, He is simply crowning His own gifts.

Because God wants those who seek justice and truth, He is not appeased by just anyone's sacrifice. Only those who truly love and fear God are able to merit His forgiveness.[42] Unrepentant sinners have the opposite effect, as Scripture says, "The sacrifice of the wicked is an abomination to the LORD."[43] While many men in the Old Testament (such as Noah, Job, and Moses) were able to appease God's anger at sin through prayer and sacrifice, they could appease God only temporarily. Because they, too, were sinners, they could not offer the complete propitiation for that sin.

This is why, in some cases, God's anger could not be appeased even by righteous men. When Israel's apostasy reached its nadir, the Lord declared through the prophet Ezekiel:

"... even if Noah, Daniel, and Job were in it, as I live, says the Lord GOD, they would deliver neither son nor daughter; they would deliver but their own lives by their righteousness."[44]

The Lord also declared through Jeremiah:

"Though Moses and Samuel stood before me, yet my heart would not turn toward this people. Send them out of my sight, and let them go!"

— JER 15:1

Because Jesus was a divine being without sin, He alone was equipped to offer God the most perfect sacrifice for sin.[45] Only

---

[42] "Merit" means deserving justly. Strictly speaking, man can merit nothing from God for, as Paul says, "Who has given a gift to him that he might be repaid?" (Rom 11:35). Nevertheless, when we become God's children in baptism, God wills that we merit His blessings under the auspices of His grace. If man could not merit (or demerit), then there would be no just rewards (or punishments).

[43] Prov 15:8; 21:27.

[44] Ezek 14:20; see also Ezek 14:14.

[45] When Satan deceived Adam and Eve into committing the Original Sin, he knew that God would not destroy them, for if He did, God would have

the eternal God made flesh could counterbalance the eternal punishment for sin by the sacrifice of Himself. Thus, Scripture teaches that Jesus' sacrifice on the Cross was the *ultimate* propitiation for sin. The Apostle John says, "And he is the *propitiation* for our sins, and not ours only but also for the whole world."[46] Only Jesus Christ, an infinite being without sin, could offer the suitable sacrifice to appease God's anger and preserve His honor and holiness. Jesus made the Father an offer that He could not refuse, and the Father accepted the offer by raising Jesus from the dead.

Yet it was the voluntary nature of Jesus' sacrifice that truly merited the Father's pity and forgiveness. Jesus said:

> "For this reason the Father loves me, because I lay down my life, that I may take it again. No one takes it from me, but I lay it down of my own accord."
>
> — JN 10:17-18

Jesus loved the Father and us so much that He was willing to become man and lay down His life for our salvation. Jesus' voluntary offering was the greatest act of love that He could show both the Father and the human race. Jesus said, "Greater love has no man than this, that a man lay down his life for his friends" (Jn 15:13).[47]

---

admitted defeat. He also knew that no sinful human being would be able to offer God a suitable sacrifice to appease His anger against sin and adequately satisfy the demands of His justice. Therefore, Satan thought that he could live in eternal rebellion against God, with his own counter-kingdom for eternity. As intelligent as Satan was, he never contemplated that God would become Man. Through the Incarnation, God would find the suitable sacrifice in His Son's death, restore man to grace, and destroy Satan's kingdom forever.

[46] 1 Jn 2:1.

[47] Aquinas says, "Christ's voluntary suffering was such a good act that, because of its being found in human nature, God was appeased for every offense of the human race with regard to those who are made one with the crucified Christ" (*Summa Theologica*, III, Q. 49, Art. 4).

Indeed, the Cross was the most suitable way that God's anger could have been averted and His love for humanity manifested. Because God's will is perfect, He would ask for the most perfect means of atonement. Jesus pleaded with the Father in the Garden of Gethsemane, "My Father, if it be possible, let this cup pass from me; nevertheless, not as I will, but as thou wilt."[48] The Father answered Jesus' plea. He willed nothing less than Jesus' sacrifice to appease His justice and reveal His love, and Jesus was perfectly obedient to His Father's will.

In God, then, we see perfect justice and perfect mercy. In His justice, He punishes sin. In His mercy, He forgives sin. Scripture reveals that God relents of His punishment (justice) and bestows His forgiveness (mercy) *through the process of propitiation*. Because Adam's sin brought eternal death, God could grant eternal life only through the perfect righteousness of Jesus Christ.

Jesus' propitiatory sacrifice was prophesied in Is 53:10-11:

> Yet it was the will of the LORD to bruise him; he has put him to grief; when he makes himself an offering for sin, he shall see his offspring, he shall prolong his days; the will of the LORD shall prosper in his hand; he shall see the fruit of the travail of his soul *and be satisfied*.

This is an amazing passage. Isaiah says that it was God's *will* to sacrifice Christ. Some translations say that it *pleased* the Lord to bruise Him.[49] God willed to see Christ's sacrifice because God willed our salvation. Since He couldn't just ignore Adam's sin and its ugly consequences, He required appeasement. God demanded His worth to be acknowledged and His honor maintained. Only then would He forgive man his sins and offer him another chance at eternal life.

---

[48] Mt 26:39; Mk 14:36; Lk 22:42.
[49] See the King James Version, New American Standard Bible, and American Standard Version.

PROPITIATION IN THE OLD TESTAMENT

The Old Testament is full of examples where God's anger is propitiated by righteous men who were zealous for God's honor and justice. God would look with *grace* upon those who had *faith* in Him as a loving Father and relent of His punishment through their sacrifices. We see this with such men as Job, Abraham, Moses, Phineas, and David.

Job

Scripture describes Job as a man who was "blameless and upright, one who feared God and turned away from evil."[50] Job was the father of ten children and a wealthy man who had many possessions. Because he loved and feared God, Job would offer sacrifices to God on behalf of his family to atone for their sins. Job had a special relationship with God.

But Satan challenged Job's special status with God; he bet the Lord that Job would curse Him if He took away all that Job had. God knew how strong Job's faith was, so He called Satan's bluff. God allowed Satan to destroy Job's family and possessions so long as he did not lay a hand on Job at first. Later, God allowed Satan to afflict Job with a terrible skin disease. In spite of his tremendous suffering, Job proved God right. Job did not sin or charge God with any wrongdoing. Instead, he praised God as he said, "The LORD gave, and the LORD has taken away; blessed be the name of the LORD" (Job 1:21).

After Satan levied the afflictions, Job was visited by three friends — Eliphaz, Bildad, and Zophar — who came to Job to console him. But, in the process, the three friends attributed Job's sufferings to his sinfulness and urged him to repent. These accusations enraged God, who declared to Eliphaz:

---

[50] Job 1:1; see also Job 1:8; 2:3.

My wrath is kindled against you and against your two friends; for you have not spoken of me what is right, as my servant Job has. Now therefore take seven bulls and seven rams, and go to my servant Job, and offer up for yourselves a burnt offering; and my servant Job shall pray for you, for I will accept his prayer not to deal with you according to your folly.

— JOB 42:7-8

The three friends went to Job and did as the Lord commanded. Job offered the prayers and sacrifices for his friends, and God accepted Job's offerings. In addition, God restored the fortunes of Job to twice as much as he had before (Job 42:9-10).

This passage clearly demonstrates how God becomes angry at sin and is propitiated by sacrifice. God expresses His anger toward the three friends for not upholding His honor and speaking falsely. To appease His wrath against their sin, God demands the friends to solicit Job to offer a blood sacrifice. Further, God requires that Job intercede for the friends. It is only through Job's prayers and sacrifices that God relents of His wrath against the friends.

Abraham

Abraham was another man of the Old Testament who had complete faith in God. When God called Abraham out of Haran to journey to the Promised Land, Abraham listened to Him. When God promised Abraham a natural heir in his old age, Abraham believed Him. And when God asked Abraham to sacrifice his son Isaac, Abraham obeyed Him. Because of his supreme faith, God viewed Abraham as a "righteous" man.[51]

During Abraham's life, God became intensely angry at the men of the city of Sodom because of their grave sin of homosex-

---

[51] See, for example, Gen 15:6.

uality.[52] Scripture says that "the men of Sodom were wicked, great sinners against the Lord" (Gen 13:13). Because of their wickedness, God threatened to destroy the Sodomites.

Because of his personal relationship with God, Abraham was able to plead with God not to execute His judgment if he could find "fifty righteous people in the city" (v. 24). Abraham's status with God prompted Him to listen to that proposal, and eventually, God agreed not to destroy Sodom if Abraham could find "ten righteous people" (v. 32). In other words, if Abraham could find enough people that were zealous for God's honor, God would relent of His wrath.

Abraham's pleadings temporarily staved off God's anger against the Sodomites. However, as we know, Abraham was unable to find even "ten righteous people" in Sodom. Because Abraham could not live up to his end of the bargain, God rained fire and brimstone upon the city of Sodom, killing all of its inhabitants (Gen 19:24).[53] While Abraham was not ultimately able to avert God's anger, the story again shows how God's anger at sin can be thwarted by righteous men.

Moses

Some of the most striking examples of propitiation occur during God's dealings with Moses. Moses was a very holy man who had an intimate relationship with God. God was pleased with Moses' life and called him by name. Scripture even says

---

[52] See Gen 19:5, where the Sodomites seek to have homosexual intercourse (sodomy) with two angels that they mistake for men as they say, "Bring them out to us, that we may know them." The word "know" (Hebrew, *yadah*) means to have intercourse (see Gen 4:25; 19:8). This proves that the Sodomites were committing the sin of homosexual intercourse, and not the supposed sin of "inhospitality" which is often argued by liberal exegetes.

[53] The Scriptures affirm that the Sodomites are suffering eternal punishments for their sin of homosexuality (2 Pet 2:6; Jude 7).

that "the LORD used to speak to Moses face to face, as a man speaks to his friend" (Gen 33:11).

Nevertheless, Moses did something that enraged God. Moses broke God's covenant by failing to circumcise his firstborn son, Gershom. Circumcision was the sign of God's covenant with His people, and Moses had disregarded it.[54] Because of Moses' infidelity, Scripture records that "the LORD met him and sought to kill him" (Ex 4:24). This is a powerful example of how God deals with violators of His covenant.

To appease the wrath of God, Moses' wife Zipporah took a flint and cut off her son's foreskin, and touched Moses' feet with the bloody flesh (Ex 4:25).[55] Zipporah's actions acknowledged God's worth and propitiated His anger toward Moses' sin. As a result, God did not kill Moses as He intended, but left him alone.

God then used Moses to lead the Israelites out of the slavery of Egypt. After their exodus, however, they fell into the sin of idolatry. When Moses left the Israelites to meet with God on Mount Sinai, they became impatient. Believing that God and Moses had abandoned them in the desert, they melted down their gold, made a calf, and worshiped it (Ex 32:2-4). God was so furious at the Israelites for their sin that He wanted to destroy their entire nation right on the spot. He said, "Now therefore let me alone, that my wrath may burn hot against them and I may consume them" (Ex 32:10).

To spare his people and preserve God's honor and justice, Moses told the Israelites: "You have sinned a great sin. And now I will go up to the Lord; perhaps I can make atonement for your sin" (Ex 32:30). Moses then propitiated God's anger by offering Him a sacrifice of fasting and prayer. Moses explained:

---

[54] See Gen 17:11 and Rom 4:11.
[55] Notice the covenantal language Zipporah uses: "You are a bridegroom of blood to me!" (Ex 4:25).

"Then I lay prostrate before the LORD as before, forty days and forty nights; I neither ate bread nor drank water, because of all the sin which you had committed, in doing what was evil in the sight of the LORD, to provoke him to anger. For I was afraid of the anger and hot displeasure which the LORD bore against you, so that he was ready to destroy you. But the LORD hearkened to me that time also."[56]

As a result of Moses' sacrifice, God did not destroy the nation of Israel. Scripture says: "And the LORD repented of the evil which he thought to do to his people" (Ex 32:14). This is another incredible example of how God wills to be propitiated to relent of His anger and forgive sinners.[57] God expresses His anger and threatens punishment, and responds to the sacrifice of a righteous person and relents of His punishment.[58]

Phineas

Before too long, Israel would again fall into the sin of idolatry and sexual perversion. While at Shittim, the Israelites engaged in orgies with Moabite women and bowed down to their false gods (Num 25:1-3). The anger of the Lord burned fiercely against the Israelites, and God commanded Moses to hang the chiefs of the people in broad daylight so that His anger would be appeased (Num 25:3-4). Moses appeased God's anger by ordering the judges to slay all those who worshiped the Baal of Peor.

---

[56] Deut 9:18-19. Moses describes offering the same sacrifice in Deut 9:25-29.

[57] When the Scriptures record instances where God threatens punishment, is appeased, and then relents of His punishment, this implies no change in God. As we have said, God is immutable and cannot change. Instead, these passages reveal that the relationship between God and the sinner has changed, and this is because God has moved the sinner by His grace to make a suitable satisfaction to appease His anger and restore justice.

[58] Moses' intercession on behalf of God's Old Covenant people foreshadows the propitiatory intercession of Jesus Christ on behalf of God's New Covenant people.

During this incident, an Israelite man named Zimri defied God and Moses with a shocking display of sinful behavior. While Moses and the people were pleading for God's mercy, Zimri, in front of the entire assembly, took a Midianite woman named Cozbi into the tent of meeting (where God would often appear in His glory cloud) to have sexual intercourse with her. A man named Phineas, who was in the priestly line of Aaron, witnessed this exhibition of immorality and defiance. Angered by what he saw, Phineas took a spear, went into the tent of meeting, and killed the couple (Num 25:7-8).

Immediately thereafter, God caused the plague that was afflicting the Israelites to cease and declared to Moses:

> "Phinehas the son of Eleazar, son of Aaron the priest, has turned back my wrath from the people of Israel, in that he was jealous with my jealousy among them, so that I did not consume the people of Israel in my jealousy. Therefore say, 'Behold, I give to him my covenant of peace; and it shall be to him, and to his descendants after him, the covenant of a perpetual priesthood, because he was jealous for his God, and made atonement for the people of Israel.'"[59]

This is another example of how righteous people can propitiate God's anger. Phineas averted God's *wrath* by making atonement for the Israelites because he was *jealous* for God's honor. Because Phineas was a righteous man who sought to preserve God's honor, he was able to appeal to God's nature, and God responded with mercy. God answers Phineas by stopping the plague and rewarding Phineas with a "covenant of peace" and "perpetual priesthood."[60]

---

[59] Num 25:11-13.

[60] We note the compelling parallels between Phineas and Christ. Like Phineas, Christ was zealous for God's honor (Jn 2:17); propitiated God's anger through sacrifice (1 Jn 2:2); made atonement for His people's sins through the

David

David is another Old Testament figure who had a special relationship with God. God even describes David as "a man after his own heart" (1 Sam 13:14). However, during David's reign as king of Israel, he lost faith in God's ability to protect his army against Israel's enemies. Knowing that David feared his army lacked sufficient troops, Satan incited David to take a census of his army in complete contempt for God. Acknowledging that he had put his trust in Satan and not God, David cried out to God:

> "I have sinned greatly in that I have done this thing. But now, I pray thee, take away the iniquity of thy servant; for I have done very foolishly."
>
> — 1 CHRON 21:8

God became enraged at David's sin. For his punishment, God gave David three choices: three years of famine, three months of devastation by his enemies, or three days of God's destructive sword. David chose "to fall into the hand of the LORD, for his mercy is very great, but let me not fall into the hand of man" (1 Chron 21:13). Thus, God sent a pestilence upon Israel, killing seventy thousand men.

Not sufficiently appeased, God sent an angel to Israel to destroy the city. However, the anticipated devastation was so severe, Scripture says:

> The LORD saw, and he repented of the evil; and he said to the destroying angel, "It is enough; now stay your hand."
>
> —1 CHRON 21:15

This language reminds us of how God expressed regret over His creation during the time of Noah, where it "grieved him to

---

shedding of blood (1 Jn 1:7); was rewarded with an everlasting priesthood (Heb 7:24); and brought His people a covenant of peace (Jn 14:27).

his heart." The language also reminds us of the golden calf incident, where Moses pleads with God by reminding Him of His promise: "And the LORD repented of the evil which he thought to do to his people" (Ex 32:14).

At this point, the angel appeared to David and commanded him to build an altar of sacrifice to God, so that the propitiation would stave off further destruction. Scripture records:

> And David built an altar to the LORD and presented burnt offerings and peace offerings, and called upon the LORD, and he answered him with fire from heaven upon the altar of burnt offering. Then the LORD commanded the angel; and he put his sword back into its sheath.
>
> — 1 CHRON 21:26-27

This is another striking example of God's personal offense at sin and how He can be appeased by sacrifice. Because of God's honor and integrity, He would not ignore David's sin. Yet, because He loved David, God gave David a choice in determining his punishment. When God meted out His punishment through the avenging angel, Scripture says God actually became grieved over its devastating effects and commanded the angel to cease. Thereafter, at the angel's command, David offered blood sacrifices to God, begging God to cease and desist from issuing any further punishments.

These brief examples give us some insight into the mystery of who God is and how He deals with us. God is a personal being who is offended by sin and wills to forgive by sacrifice. Those who sin against God merit His wrath, and those who love God and seek to preserve His honor merit His mercy. As we have seen, Noah "found favor" with God, Job was "upright and blameless," Abraham was "righteous," Moses spoke to God "as a friend," Phineas was "jealous for his God," and David was a man "after God's own heart." Because of their status with God, these men could beseech God to forgive sin, although incompletely and imperfectly. It would take God's sinless and divine Son to serve as the ultimate propitiation for sin.

Ritual Sacrifices

The Old Testament sacrifices were not only spontaneous offerings to avert God's ensuing wrath and implore His forgiveness. Offering sacrifice to God was part of humanity since the dawn of creation.[61] God may have taught Adam how to sacrifice animals after He clothed Adam and Eve with "garments of skins" (Gen 3:21). The first recorded activity of Adam's sons, Cain and Abel, was about their sacrifices to God (Gen 4:3-5). Because Abel's sacrifice was from the first fruits of his flock but Cain's was not, God was pleased with Abel's sacrifice but not Cain's (Gen 4:4-5).

When Noah sacrificed to God after the flood, the sacrifice pleased God so much that God promised never to destroy the earth again (Gen 8:21). Job offered sacrifices to God on behalf of his children for even the mere possibility that they might have sinned (Job 1:5). Abraham also offered many sacrifices to God,[62] as did his son Isaac and grandson Jacob.[63] Well before the golden calf incident, after which God greatly increased the requirement to offer sacrifices to appease Him, the Israelites would "offer sacrifice to God."[64]

When God added the Levites to the priesthood, He formalized ritual sacrifices by requiring sin offerings, guilt offerings, burnt offerings, grain offerings, thank offerings, and peace offerings.[65] These sacrifices were offered under the administration

---

[61] Man's conviction to offer sacrifice to God was part of the worship laws that God wrote on the minds and hearts of men. See Rom 1:19-23; 2:14-15; Acts 17:24-31.

[62] Gen 12:7-8; 13:4, 18.

[63] Gen 26:24-25; 31:54; 35:1-7; 46:1.

[64] See Ex 3:18; 5:3, 8.

[65] See, for example, Lev 1-16.

of Israel, to remind the Israelites of their sinfulness and God's holiness. These offerings, which would ascend as "an aroma pleasing to the Lord," would show appreciation for God, appease His wrath and make temporary atonement for the sins of the people of Israel.[66]

As we have discussed, these Old Testament ritual sacrifices involved the shedding of animal blood. The blood would be presented to God in the tent of meeting, thrown against the altar, placed on the horns of the altar, sprinkled before the veil of the sanctuary, rubbed onto the finger of the priest, and even thrown on to the people.[67] These blood sacrifices drew their power from the anticipated blood-sacrifice of Christ.

When God saw the blood of these sacrifices, He would see the future bloodshed of His Son. Because Jesus' sacrifice was secured "before the foundation of the world" (Apoc 13:8), God could apply the merits of His atoning blood to the Old Covenant sacrifices. Nevertheless, these were imperfect sacrifices that would appease God's wrath only momentarily, and only because they foreshadowed the sacrifice of Christ.

The power of blood sacrifice is particularly evident in the account of the first Passover sacrifice, during Israel's exodus from Egypt. God required every Israelite family to sacrifice an unblemished lamb and paint the blood of the lamb on its doorposts. Moses reveals:

> "For the LORD will pass through to slay the Egyptians; and when he sees the blood on the lintel and on the two door-

---

[66] See, for example, Gen 8:21; Lev 1:9, 13, 17, 2:2, 9, 12; 3:5, 16; 4:31; 6:15, 21; 8:21, 28; 17:6; 23:13, 18; Num 15:3, 7, 10, 13-14, 24; 18:17; 28:2, 6, 8, 13, 24, 27; 29:2, 6, 8, 13, 36; Eph 5:2; Phil 4:18; 2 Cor 2:15; 1 Pet 2:5.

[67] See, for example, Ex 23:18; 24:6, 8; 29:12, 16, 20-21; 30:10; 34:25; Lev 1:5, 11, 15; 3:2, 8, 13, 17; 4:5-7, 16-18, 25, 30, 34; 6:27, 30; 7:2, 14, 26-27, 33; 8:15, 19, 23-24, 30; 9:9, 12, 18; 10:18; 12:4-5, 7; 14:6, 14, 17, 25, 28, 51-52; 15:19, 25; 16:14-15; 16:15, 18-19, 27.

posts, the LORD will pass over the door, and will not allow the destroyer to enter your houses to slay you."

— Ex 12:23

When God saw the blood of the lambs, He spared Israel's firstborn sons, for God saw in that blood the blood of the true Lamb of God, sprinkled on the wood of the Cross.[68]

PROTESTANT MISCONCEPTIONS ABOUT THE ATONEMENT

Anger and Anthropomorphisms

In the face of Scripture's clear teaching that God gets angry and desires to be appeased, many Protestants argue that Scripture's descriptions of God's anger are mere anthropomorphisms — that is, projections of human qualities onto God — and that God doesn't really have anger.[69] If God doesn't have anger, then, the Protestant concludes, there is no need to appease Him by the sacrifice of the Mass. This view is misleading and, ultimately, erroneous. It is true that God's anger is not like human anger. This is because human anger is a passion, and God does not have passions or emotions.[70] God is altogether simple, perfect, and immutable. Speaking absolutely, then, Scripture's attribution of anger to God is metaphorical.[71]

---

[68] See also Ex 24:4-11; 29:19-21; Num 22:39-23:12 and 2 Kings 3:27 for other examples of the inherent power of blood sacrifice.

[69] Examples of anthropomorphisms include God referring to the apple of His "eye" (Deut 32:10) or His "holy arm" (Ps 98:1; Is 52:10).

[70] Anger, like all emotions, requires passivity and potentiality (that is, the ability to change). Because God cannot change, He cannot have emotions. As Aquinas teaches, God is pure act with no potentiality because, absolutely speaking, actuality is prior to potentiality (something can change from potentiality to actuality only by a being in actuality, and God is the First Being).

[71] We say "metaphorical" because there is a likeness or analogy between human and divine anger, but there are also vast differences. They are neither purely equivocal nor univocal.

However, it is one thing to say that God's anger is different than ours and quite another to say that God has no anger at all. Such an attempt to reclassify God's anger as solely anthropomorphic — and thus, in reality, nonexistent— denies the plain meaning of Scripture.[72] Since God is the author of Scripture and cannot lie, it is important to take His words at face value: God means what He says. Because Scripture shows that God actually *verbalizes* His anger, we have to conclude that His anger must exist, lest we accuse God of deceiving us.[73] The fact that punitive justice often follows God's declaration of anger also proves that His anger is real.[74] Moreover, God's anger is real in that when it is appeased, He may respond with mercy.[75]

Many hesitate to attribute anger to God because they confuse it with human anger. As we said above, God's anger is not an emotional matter of "flying off the handle." Rather, Scripture's descriptions of God's anger express God's will to punish sin and restore justice.[76] In other words, God's anger is a manifestation of divine justice. It expresses the vengeance God takes against those who oppose His will, but it is always directed to the good. Speaking in human terms, we might say that God's anger is perfectly righteous

---

[72] While Protestants claim that the Scriptures are clear and self-interpreting, they often deny the plain meaning of the Scriptures. For example, they deny that Peter is the rock of the Church (Mt 16:18); that we must eat Jesus' flesh and drink His Blood to have eternal life (Jn 6:51-58); that the apostles and their successors have the authority to forgive sins (Jn 20:23; Jas 5:14-15); that baptism saves us from sin (1 Pet 3:21); and that a man is justified by works and not by faith alone (Jas 2:24).

[73] See, for example, Mal 2:16; Ezek 25:14; Heb 4:3; see also Rom 1:18; 2:5, 8; 3:5; 9:22, where God's wrath is personalized in the active voice.

[74] See, for example, Gen 6:5-7; 7:6; 18:20; 19:24; Num 11:1; 12:9-10; 1 Kings 11:9-11; Is 10:5-6.

[75] See, for example, Num 11:10; 25:1-13; Deut 9:8, 19-20; Ps 2:12; 78:38.

[76] For God, anger is in the will because anger is attached to justice and God wills justice; for humans, anger is a passion of the sensitive appetite (and God doesn't have a sensitive appetite).

and suited to His divine nature. Unlike human anger, God's anger has nothing malicious, spiteful, or arbitrary about it. It is always rational and predictable because it is provoked by evil alone, and not injured pride, as is often the case with human beings.

From a Catholic perspective, the Bible's descriptions of God's anger cannot be merely anthropomorphic because Christ's offering to appease the anger is real. Because Christ truly offered Himself on the Cross, God truly must have been angry at Adam's sin (that is, Adam must have truly opposed God's will and violated His justice). God's condemnation of the entire human race underscores how angry God was. Further, because God has really opened to us the gates of heaven in spite of Adam's sin, He must have really been appeased by Christ's offering.

The Atonement as a "Penal Substitution"

Many Protestants also use the "anthropomorphic" description of God's anger to support a common view of the Atonement as a legal or forensic transaction. This is often called the "penal substitution" theory.[77] If the Atonement is a mere legal transaction where Christ impersonally pays the debt for sin by suffering in our stead, then a personal, propitiatory sacrifice to appease God's anger (i.e., the Mass) is unnecessary.

First, however, putting the Atonement exclusively in a legal context misses the essence of "covenant." As we have learned, the parties to a covenant relationship enjoy the benefits of mutual love and forgiveness. If one party breaches the terms of the covenant, the other party still loves the offender and is bound to show him mercy. In a legal arrangement, there are no provisions for love, concern, or forgiveness. A criminal defendant is convicted or freed based upon the letter of the law, not the love and mercy of the

---

[77] Though Protestants have many different theories about the Atonement, the "penal substitution" theory is a most common one.

judge. In the New Covenant, Christ's atoning work is an act of gracious mercy, not legal acquittal. This is why Paul tells the Romans, "You are not under law but under grace" (Rom 6:14).

Second, if the penal substitution theory were true, God would legally owe us salvation, and no one would go to hell. That is because God, being perfectly just, would not require two payments for the same sin. We know that this cannot be true, however, because Jesus said people would go to hell.[78] In fact, if Christ paid the eternal penalty for our sins, He would be suffering in hell for eternity. Thus, the Protestant doctrine of "penal substitution" is nothing more than a theological fiction.

Protestants may counter by saying that Jesus' payment for our sins is effective only when a person accepts that payment in faith. However, if the Atonement were purely a legal transaction, then faith would not be required at all, because faith is not a dimension of law. (A convicted criminal's faith in his sentencing judge has no bearing on the prison term he receives.) Rather, faith is a dimension of covenant relationships, particularly within the context of family. Hence, Christ's Atonement is not an impersonal legal motion to a judge to pardon a criminal, but a personal plea to the Father to forgive the sinner. Christ doesn't free us like defendants from prison, but reconciles us as sons and daughters to our heavenly Father. The Atonement is about personal propitiation, not legal pardon.

Nevertheless, for the sake of argument, let's agree that a person accepts Jesus' payment in faith and is acquitted of his sins. He accepts Jesus into his life as his personal Lord and Savior and goes on to live a life of Christian virtue. Ten years later, however, that same person experiences tragedy: he loses his wife and children in a fatal car crash. He loses his faith in Christ and gets involved in drugs and prostitution. If that person was acquitted of his sins ten

---

[78] Mt 5:29-30; 7:13; 10:28; 18:9; 23:15, 33; Mk 9:43, 45, 47; Lk 12:5.

years ago, as the Protestant contends, he would still be destined for heaven (even though Scripture says that drunkards and fornicators shall not inherit the kingdom of heaven).[79]

So how do we reconcile the contradiction? The only logical rebuttal to this hypothetical scenario is to say that the person was never saved in the first place. That is, the Protestant must argue that such a person never truly accepted Christ's substitute payment in faith. Even though he had been living a life of grace and virtue before his tragedy, the Protestant must argue that the person never had "true" or "saving" faith.

A major problem with this argument is that it is impossible to live virtuously without God's saving grace; if the person was never saved, therefore, he in effect managed to accomplish the impossible prior to "losing" his faith.

But a greater problem with this particular argument is that Scripture *never* makes a distinction between "true faith" and "false faith," and never teaches that a person who has saving grace will persevere in that grace to the end of his life. To the contrary, Scripture repeatedly teaches that a person can have true and genuine faith in God, yet lose his faith through sin.[80] This reveals the flaw inherent in the doctrine of a Christian's certainty regarding his salvation: the Protestant Christian who believes in "penal substitution" can never know he has truly been "acquitted" of his sins until the day he dies. Because Scripture is clear that true Christians can fall away from the faith and lose the life of grace, he therefore can never know whether he has truly received Christ's legal payment in authentic, saving faith. When the only distinction between a "saved" and an "un-saved" Christian is that the former will persevere and the latter will not, and it is a given that no one can predict his future, this necessarily imposes upon the Protestant uncertainty about his salvation until the end of his life,

---

[79] 1 Cor 5:11; 6:10; Eph 5:5; Apoc 21:8; 22:15.
[80] See Rom 4:15; Gal 3:10.

and directly contradicts Protestantism's oft-repeated mantra of being "once saved, always saved."

For Catholics, we hope and have confident assurance in our salvation (Rom 8:24) so long as we persevere to the end of our lives, as Jesus teaches.[81] That means Catholics know salvation is ours to lose. By contrast, Protestants who are "once saved, always saved" through the "substitute sacrifice" of Christ cannot be sure whether salvation is even theirs to begin with.

God's Gift of Grace

The Protestant idea of accepting Jesus' payment for sin by having faith in Him brings up additional thoughts on the Catholic Church's teaching on grace. Protestants contend that a person must have faith in Christ's once-for-all sacrifice on the Cross to be saved, and that nothing more is needed. Many Protestants claim that a person's works are irrelevant to this process, for there is nothing that a person can do to please God. Because God is perfection, our imperfect works can never secure His favor. To the Protestant, this makes offering the Mass — or any other "work" to further our salvation — an affront to God, worthy of His condemnation.

Before we address the sacrifice of the Mass, we need to point out that this particular Protestant position is clearly duplicitous. If a person's *works* cannot please God, then that person's *faith* cannot please God, either. Both are imperfect. The truth is that *neither faith nor works* can please our perfect God outside of His grace. This is because all men, prior to repentance and baptism, are under the Old Covenant curse of eternal death for their sins. We are all born under the condemnation "of the law." It is only when a man responds to God's actual grace that the judgment of law is removed. Grace is a free and unmerited gift from God,

---

[81] Mt 10:22, 24:13; Mk 13:13.

which He makes available to man because of the sacrifice of Christ. There is nothing man can do to merit grace; he can only freely respond to and cooperate with it.

A man responds to God's grace by repenting of his sins and being baptized into Jesus Christ. When this happens, God removes man from the Old Covenant system of law, and man enters into the New Covenant system of grace (Rom 5:1-2). In Baptism, by virtue of the sacrifice of Christ, God forgives man his sins, infuses his soul with *sanctifying grace*, and makes him a child of God. Faith, therefore, is the first step to grace, without which it is impossible to please God (Heb 11:6). However, a man must respond to God's grace with both faith *and works*, and not faith alone (Jas 2:24). As James teaches, "Faith without works is dead" (Jas 2:26).

Once man is in the state of grace, he is able to have a gracious relationship with God. Because God views man through grace and not law, man is able to please God with both faith and works, as Scripture clearly teaches.[82] If a man does not respond to God's actual graces in Christ, Christ's sacrifice is no benefit to him. He remains under God's condemnation in the system of law and can have no hope of eternal life. This is why Jesus said, "He who believes in him is not condemned; he who does not believe is condemned *already*, because he has not believed in the name of the only Son of God" (Jn 3:18).

Because grace is infused or "poured" into a person's soul, grace is not a mere state of relationship with God (Rom 5:2, 5). Grace is also a power residing in the person that theologians often call "ontic" grace.[83] This indwelling of grace renews our

---

[82] See, for example, 1 Cor 1:21; 7:32; 2 Cor 5:9; Col 3:20; 1 Thess 2:4; 4:1; Heb 11:5-6; 1 Jn 3:22.

[83] "Ontic" comes from the word "ontology," which is the study of being or existence. For examples of ontic grace, see Acts 4:33; 6:8; 13:43; Rom 1:5; 5:2, 17, 20; 12:3, 6; 15:15; 1 Cor 1:4; 3:10; 15:10; 2 Cor 1:12; 4:15; 6:1; 9:14; 12:9; Gal 2:9; Eph 1:6; 3:2, 7-8; 4:7, 29; Phil 1:7; 2 Thess 1:12; 1 Tim 1:14; 2 Tim 1:9; 2 Tim 2:1; Heb 12:15; 13:9; Jas 4:6; 1 Pet 4:10; 5:5; 2 Pet 1:2; 3:18; Jude 1:4.

wounded nature to be conformed to God's perfect nature and moves us to produce faith and works that are pleasing to God.[84] As we will see in the next chapter, God's grace is available continually because Christ continually presents His sacrifice to God in heaven. Without Christ's sacrifice, there is no grace; without grace, there is no salvation.

Grace and Sacrifice

This discussion of grace poses another challenge to Protestant theology. As we have learned, God began implementing the New Covenant with Adam and Eve. In this new arrangement, God would grant grace and mercy to those who approached Him personally with faith. If God required *faith* to enter into His Old Covenant, why did He require ritual blood sacrifices from his faithful as well?

If Protestant theology is correct, then the ritual sacrifices offered by such faithful men as Abel, Noah, Job, Abraham, Moses, and David would have offended God and brought about a loss in their justification. After all, these men were ultimately justified by the sacrifice of Christ. However, we know that the sacrifices these men offered did *not* offend God because Paul says in his letter to the Hebrews that these men were justified by grace through faith, and have received their eternal reward (Heb 11:16). Protestants cannot explain why these men, who were justified by faith in God in the Old Covenant, continued to offer blood sacrifices to God with God's favor and approval.

The Protestant position becomes especially problematic when we look at Abraham's sacrifice of Isaac. Even though Abraham was already justified in the eyes of God (Gen 15:6; Heb 11:10), God required Abraham to sacrifice his son. Further, James

---

[84] See my book *The Biblical Basis for the Catholic Faith*, pages 179-185, for a discussion on grace and how grace interiorly renews a person's wounded nature.

states that Abraham's offering of Isaac was an act that justified him (Jas 2:21-24). Specifically, James says that Abraham's faith was completed by his offering of Isaac (Jas 2:22). We can only conclude that Abraham's sacrifice *maintained and perfected* his justification. In fact, it was only after Abraham's sacrifice that God swore an oath to Abraham promising him and his descendants covenant blessings.[85]

If men who were justified by grace in the Old Covenant offered sacrifices to God to maintain their justification, *then the same process can and does take place in the New Covenant.* The only difference is that the grace God offered in the Old Covenant was based on Christ's anticipated sacrifice, and the grace God offers in the New Covenant is based on Christ's ongoing sacrifice. The sacrifice of the Mass, foreshadowed in the Old Covenant and consummated in the New Covenant, *never ceases.* As we will see in the next section, this is exactly what was prophesied by Jeremiah and Malachi.

---

[85] Gen 22:16-18; Heb 6:13-18.

CHAPTER II

The Eternal Sacrifice
of Jesus Christ

PROPHECIES OF CHRIST'S ETERNAL SACRIFICE

Jeremiah was the first to prophesy about both Christ's eternal sacrifice and the sacrificial priesthood of the New Covenant. At this moment in history (around 625 B.C.), God was severely punishing Israel for its sins. The Jews had already divided into two nations. Moreover, the northern nation, Israel, had been conquered by the Assyrians; and, Jeremiah predicted that Judah, the southern nation, would soon be handed over to the Babylonians (Jer 20:4-6).[1] It was against this backdrop that God promised the world a New and Everlasting Covenant through the sacrifice of Jesus Christ.

God revealed through Jeremiah that He would raise up a "Righteous Branch" from the line of David and His name would be "The Lord is our righteousness."[2] Through this Messiah, God would "make a new covenant with the house of Israel and the house of Judah."[3] In this New Covenant, God reveals:

---

[1] In 931 B.C., Israel divided into two nations, the northern (Judah) nation and the southern (Israel) nation. Assyria conquered Israel in 722 B.C., and Babylon conquered Judah in 586 B.C..

[2] Jer 23:5-6; 33:15-16.

[3] Jer 31:31; Jer 31:32-34; 32:40. Jeremiah is especially significant because he is the only prophet to use the phrase "New Covenant."

> For thus says the LORD: David shall never lack a man to sit
> on the throne of the house of Israel, and the Levitical priests
> shall never lack a man in my presence to offer burnt offer-
> ings, to burn cereal offerings, and to make sacrifices for ever.
>   — JER 33:17-18

In the New Covenant, then, God reveals that there will be perpetual sacrifices offered by His priests. The "kingdom of David" and the "house of Israel and Judah" are metaphors for the Church. The "Levitical priests" symbolize the priests of the New Covenant who will serve under the "Righteous Branch" from the line of David.[4] These priests will present offerings and sacrifices *forever*. In addition, each mention of the words "offerings" and "sacrifices" uses the Hebrew *minchah*, which is singular. This usage alludes to the *single* sacrifice of Jesus Christ, which will be perpetually offered by His priests.

The prophet Zechariah echoes Jeremiah's prophecy. After declaring the coming of the righteous "Branch," God promises that He will set His people free "because of the blood of my covenant" (Zech 9:11).[5] Under the administration of the New Covenant, God reveals that His people will "drink blood like wine" and be saved.[6] Zechariah further reveals that God's favor

---

[4] See, for example, 2 Sam 7:13,16; 1 Chron 17:14; Ps 89:3-4; and Dan 2:44, where God promises to forever establish the kingdom of David, and Mt 1:1; 9:27; 15:22; 20:30-31; 22:40; Mk 10:47-48; Lk 1:32-33; 2:11; 3:31; 18:38-39; and Jn 1:4, 9, where God's promises are fulfilled in Jesus Christ and His universal, Catholic Church.

[5] See also Zech 6:11, where God chooses Joshua to be high priest, even though Zerubbabel was a king from the Davidic line. "Joshua" prefigures "Jesus," the High Priest of the New Covenant. This underscores the Eucharistic theme of Zechariah's revelation (e.g., priesthood, covenant, blood, wine, salvation).

[6] Zech 9:15-16. This is a clear prediction of the Eucharistic drink, in which the priests of the New Covenant change wine into the blood of Jesus Christ, and the people drink Christ's blood to be saved as He commanded (Jn 6:53-56).

upon the "house of David" will be due to the propitiatory sacrifice of the Messiah, Jesus Christ, "him whom they have pierced" (Zech 12:10).[7]

Malachi's prophecy of Christ's perpetual sacrifice, to be offered throughout the world, is even more explicit. As with Jeremiah and the other Major Prophets, God reveals through Malachi His growing displeasure with Israel's sacrifices. In fact, because Israel was sacrificing blind, sick, and lame animals and not the first fruits of their flock, God was no longer appeased by these sacrifices.[8] Israel's religion was becoming impersonal, legal ritual, and ignoring the personal dimensions of God's covenant with them. The priests were offering sacrifices not to preserve God's honor in faith, but to fulfill the minimum requirements of the law.

As a result, God chastised His priests by saying:

"If then I am a father, where is my honor? And if I am a master, where is my fear? says the LORD of hosts to you, O priests, who despise my name."

— MAL 1:6

God went on to say:

"Oh, that there were one among you who would shut the doors, that you might not kindle fire upon my altar in vain! I have no pleasure in you, says the LORD of hosts, and I will not accept an offering from your hand."

— MAL 1:10

---

[7] We again see references to covenant, the Messiah, blood, wine, the priesthood, the Church, and perpetual sacrifices in the context of Christ and the New Covenant.

[8] Mal 1:7-8, 12-14. The Jews were also divorcing their wives and marrying foreign women (Mal 2:10-17) and practicing sorcery, adultery, false swearing, and the oppression of workers, widows, and orphans (Mal 3:5). Thus, even if the Jews were sacrificing unblemished animals, they would still have been unacceptable to God. In their sinful state, the Jews were not trying to preserve God's honor and holiness, but were actually demonstrating contempt for Him.

After rejecting their faithless sacrifices, God said:

> "For from the rising of the sun to its setting my name is great among the nations, and in every place incense is offered to my name, and a pure offering; for my name is great among the nations, says the LORD of hosts."
>
> — MAL 1:11

In this prophecy, God reveals that He is going to make obsolete the system of Old Covenant sacrifices and perfect it with a new sacrifice. There are four important features about this new sacrifice:

- The sacrifice will be offered "from the rising to the setting of the sun."
- The sacrifice will be offered "in every place."
- The sacrifice will be offered "among the nations."
- The sacrifice will be a single sacrifice.

As with the "offerings" prophesied in Jeremiah, the "pure offerings" in Malachi 1:11 use the Hebrew *minchah*, which is singular.[9] Thus, Malachi is referring to a *single* sacrifice, yet it will be offered "from the rising to the setting of the sun" and "in every place."

Malachi could not have been referring to a new sacrifice under the Old Covenant because the Mosaic Law would have prohibited it.[10] In addition, he could not have been referring to

---

[9] Malachi couples the Hebrew *minchah* (offering) with *qatar* (incense) to emphasize that he was revealing a new sacrifice (see, for example, Ex 29:13, 18, 25; Lev 1:9, 13, 15, 17; 6:15, 22-23; 4:7; Deut 33:10; Is 6:6; Amos 4:5 where "incense" is associated with "sacrifice"). Even the prominent Protestant translation of the Bible, the King James Version, correctly translates *minchah* as "offering," in the singular. Further, *minchah* refers to an unbloody sacrifice in contrast with *sebach*, which refers to a bloody sacrifice.

[10] See Mal 4:4, where God commands the Jews to observe the Law of Moses; this demonstrates that God was not adding a new sacrifice to the Mosaic Law. The New Covenant sacrifice of Jesus Christ would completely abolish the Old

a sacrifice offered by the Jews, since they were not dispersed "among the nations." Those "among the nations" could refer only to the Gentiles who would be incorporated into the New Covenant established by the Messiah. Moreover, the Jews would have not understood the single, perpetual, and pure dimensions of this sacrifice in the context of their Old Covenant system.

Malachi can only be referring to the worldwide sacrifice of Jesus Christ, the "lamb without blemish" (1 Pet 1:19). The early Church Fathers were unanimous in their recognition of this universal sacrifice. It is the pure sacrifice of Christ that is sacramentally offered among the nations, around the clock and in every place, in Catholic churches throughout the world. We can only conclude that Malachi's prophecy has been fulfilled by the continual, sacramental re-presentation of Christ's pure offering in the Holy Mass, or Malachi is a false prophet.

In chapter 3, Malachi connects this new sacrifice to the New Covenant. He says:

> "Behold, I send my messenger to prepare the way before me, and the Lord whom you seek will suddenly come to his temple; the messenger of the covenant in whom you delight, behold, he is coming, says the LORD of hosts."
>
> — MAL 3:1

Like Jeremiah, Malachi refers to the coming Messiah as "Lord" who is the messenger of the "covenant."[11] Malachi says the Lord is coming to the "temple," which puts His coming in the context of offering sacrifice. This is confirmed in the next two verses:

Covenant Law (see 2 Cor 3:14; Heb 7:18; 8:7, 13; 10:9). The destruction of the Jewish Temple in A.D. 70 by Titus also made the Jewish sacrifices a thing of the past.

[11] John the Baptist is the "messenger" that prepares the way for the "Lord," who is the "messenger of the covenant."

> He will sit as a refiner and purifier of silver, and he will
> purify the sons of Levi and refine them like gold and silver,
> till they present right offerings to the LORD. Then the offer-
> ing of Judah and Jerusalem will be pleasing to the LORD as
> in the days of old and as in former years.
>
> — MAL 3:3-4

As with Jeremiah, Malachi reveals the following about the New Covenant sacrifice:

- It will be offered by the "sons of Levi";
- It will be offered by "Judah and Jerusalem";
- It will be a single offering (the two instances of "offerings" in vv. 3-4 are both the singular *minchah*).

The "sons of Levi" symbolize the priests of the New Covenant;[12] "Judah and Jerusalem" symbolizes the Church of the New Covenant, which Paul refers to as the "Israel of God."[13] In this New Israel, all the nations (both Jews and Gentiles) will gather to worship God. The priests of the Church will offer a single and perpetual sacrifice from the rising of the sun to its setting and in every place around the world. This is the pure sacrifice of Jesus Christ, offered once-for-all on the Cross and made present in the Catholic Mass.

Some non-Catholics argue that the "sons of Levi" in these prophecies cannot be referring to today's Catholic priests because the Levitical priesthood has been abolished by Christ.[14] Those

---

[12] Ezekiel also prophesies about the Levites offering sacrifices in the new Temple (Ezek 40:46; 43:19; 44:10; 45:5; 48:11). Note also that the Levites, who will offer the New Covenant sacrifice, cannot refer to Christ because "Levites" is plural, and Christ was from the tribe of Judah.

[13] See Gal 6:16; Rom 9:24; Gal 3:28. Paul also makes the connection between the New Covenant priesthood and the offering of Israel and Judah (Heb 8:7-8).

[14] See Heb 7:11-12. See also Heb 7:18; 8:7, 13; 10:9.

making these arguments fail to recognize the prophetic imagery and biblical typology inherent in these revelations.[15] The "Levitical priests" are *prototypes* of the Catholic priesthood just like, for example, Moses was a prototype of Jesus Christ, and the Passover sacrifice was a prototype of Christ's sacrifice. So, although the Levitical priesthood has been literally abolished, it carries on symbolically through the New Covenant priesthood (because of the ongoing earthly offerings of Christ's eternal sacrifice), as these prophets expressly reveal.

The prophet Isaiah also reveals that God's New Covenant sacrifice will involve the "Levites." To set the context, God first says, "I am coming to gather all nations and tongues; and they shall come and shall see my glory" (Is 66:18). When God reveals that He will gather together "all nations," He is referring to the universal, "Catholic" Church, where He will unite Jews and Gentiles in the New Covenant. God then says that "all the nations" will make an "offering to the Lord" on the "holy mountain Jerusalem," which is where Jesus established the Eucharist.[16]

After alluding to the New Covenant sacrifice of Christ, God says, "And some of them also I will take for priests *and for Levites.*"[17] We once again see the "Levites" offering sacrifice under the auspices of the New Covenant. That God says He will take only "*some* of them for priests and Levites" also denies the Protestant notion that the New Covenant priesthood refers *only* to a

---

[15] In biblical typology, a *prototype* is a person, place or thing whose pattern is fulfilled in the future. The fulfillment of the *prototype* is often called the *antitype* (e.g., Moses is a *prototype* of Jesus, and Jesus is the *anti-type* of Moses).

[16] See Is 66:19-20. In three verses, God refers five times to this universal gathering ("all nations and tongues"; "to the nations"; "lands afar off"; "among the nations"; and, "all the nations"). This underscores that God's revelation refers to the unity of the New Covenant.

[17] Is 66:21. See also the next verse (v. 22), where God refers to "the new heavens and the new earth," which is realized at the consummation of the New Covenant (Apoc 21:1).

"universal priesthood of believers." God makes a clear distinction between the ministerial priesthood and the priesthood of the laity.

The multiple references to "Judah and Jerusalem" further demonstrate that these revelations are about the Church and the sacrifice of the New Covenant. For example, Jeremiah, the only Old Testament prophet to use the phrase "New Covenant," reveals that "all nations" shall gather to worship "the Lord in Jerusalem," and then "the house of Judah shall join the house of Israel."[18] In those days, Jeremiah reveals, "Judah will be saved, and Israel will dwell securely" (Jer 23:6). As Protestants even agree, this union of Judah and Jerusalem takes place in the Church, the one Body of Christ. [19]

God also reveals through Ezekiel:

"Behold, I am about to take the stick of Joseph . . . and the tribes of Israel associated with him; and I will join it with the stick of Judah, and make them one stick, that they may be one in my hand."

— EZEK 37:19

God will do this in the New Covenant, for He then says: "I will make a covenant of peace with them; it shall be an everlasting covenant with them" (Ezek 37:26).

Zechariah also reveals, "And the Lord will inherit Judah as his portion in the holy land, and will again choose Jerusalem."[20] God then says through Zechariah that this restoration is effected by "the

---

[18] See Jer 3:17-18. See also Jer 17:24-25.

[19] Protestants believe that the restoration of "Judah and Israel" is consummated in the Christian Church, yet they deny that the Church has a sacrificial priesthood. This position is duplicitous. As revealed by the prophets and, ultimately, Christ Himself at the Last Supper, the Church and the priesthood are expressly connected. One cannot exist without the other. Paul also connects Christ's priesthood to "Israel and Judah" in the "New Covenant" by quoting from the prophet Jeremiah (Heb 8:8).

[20] Zech 2:12. See also Joel 3:1.

blood of my covenant" (Zech 9:11). These and many other Scriptures demonstrate that Jeremiah and Malachi's prophecies of a universal, perpetual sacrifice offered by "the sons of Levi" for the restoration of "Judah and Jerusalem" *must* refer to the New Covenant sacrifice of Jesus Christ. This is the sacrifice Jesus offered once-for-all on the Cross of Calvary, and makes present through the priests of His Church around the clock, and around the world, under the appearance of bread and wine in the Holy Mass.

THE PRIESTHOOD OF MELCHIZEDEK

In connection with bread and wine, there is another important Old Testament sacrifice that foreshadows the sacramental offering of Jesus Christ, and it may be the most important one of them all. That is the sacrifice of Melchizedek, who is the first priest mentioned in the Old Testament. Paul in his letter to the Hebrews repeatedly states that Jesus' priesthood is modeled after that of Melchizedek.[21] About Jesus, Paul writes:

- "Thou art a priest forever, after the order of Melchizedek" (Heb 5:6).
- . . . being designated by God a high priest after the order of Melchizedek (Heb 5:10).
- . . . having become a high priest for ever after the order of Melchizedek (Heb 6:20).
- . . . when another priest arises in the likeness of Melchizedek (Heb 7:15).

---

[21] Some modern scholars dispute whether Paul is the author of the letter to the Hebrews. The Catholic Church, however, has affirmed the Pauline authorship of the Epistle. The councils of Florence and Trent refer to "the fourteen epistles of Paul the Apostle." The Pontifical Biblical Commission in 1914 also affirmed the inspiration and Pauline origin of the Epistle. Whether Paul actually penned the letter or used an amanuensis (as he did with his letter to the Romans) is a judgment that is reserved to the Church.

- "Thou art a priest forever, after the order of Melchizedek" (Heb 7:17).

These descriptions fulfill David's prophecy about Jesus:

The Lord has sworn and will not change his mind, "You are a priest forever after the order of Melchizedek."

— Ps 110:4

We learn more about Melchizedek in the book of Genesis.

In chapter 14, Moses describes Abram (Abraham)'s victory over Chedorlaomer and the kings who had taken captive his nephew Lot. When Abram discovered that Lot had been kidnapped, he led 318 soldiers to wage war against these evil men. Although Abram's army was outnumbered in battle, he relied completely upon God to help him achieve the victory. Abram won the battle, rescued Lot and his family, and brought back the spoils to the Valley of Shaveh. Scripture records what happened next:

And Melchizedek king of Salem brought out bread and wine; he was priest of God Most High. And he blessed him and said, "Blessed be Abram by God Most High, maker of heaven and earth; and blessed be God Most High, who has delivered your enemies into your hand!" And Abram gave him a tenth of everything.

— Gen 14:18-20

There are a number of important features that demonstrate how Melchizedek's priesthood was the precursor to the priesthood of Jesus Christ. First, Melchizedek is described as the "king of Salem."[22] David reveals the future significance of Salem in Psalm 76:

---

[22] Gen 14:18. Melchizedek's title "king of Salem" may be translated as "king of righteousness" and "king of peace" (Heb 7:2). These titles foreshadow those given to Jesus Christ, the Righteous One and Prince of Peace.

> In Judah God is known, his name is great in Israel. His abode
> has been established in Salem, his dwelling place in Zion.[23]

God establishes His kingdom in Salem because it was in Salem (the future Jerusalem) where Christ founded the Church and instituted the Eucharistic sacrifice.

Second, as with Jesus, Melchizedek's priesthood was created directly by God. Melchizedek did not inherit his priesthood through legal process or family bloodline. It existed independently of the jurisdiction of the Old Covenant law. This is why Paul describes Melchizedek as "without father or mother or genealogy, and has neither beginning of days nor end of life, but resembling the Son of God he continues a priest forever."[24]

Because Melchizedek's priesthood was created by God and independent of the Mosaic Law, it continued perpetually and served as the prototype of the New Covenant priesthood. God did this by establishing Melchizedek's priesthood as a perpetual office by an oath, not by legal succession.[25] Because of this, Melchizedek's priesthood foreshadowed the manner in which New Testament priests would acquire their priesthood — through the "oath" (*sacramentum*) of Holy Orders.

Third, Melchizedek offers a sacrifice of bread and wine. This was a "thanksgiving" (in Greek, *eucharistein*) sacrifice to God for delivering Abram from his enemies. This thanksgiving sacrifice foreshadowed the Eucharistic sacrifice that Jesus would offer in Jerusalem to deliver His Church from her enemy, Satan. Just as

---

[23] Ps 76:1-2. Notice how David mentions both "Judah" and "Israel" in connection with God establishing His abode in "Salem." Once again, Judah and Israel foreshadow the Church of the New Covenant, and Salem is the future site where Jesus (the King of Jerusalem) established the New Covenant in His blood.

[24] Heb 7:3. Paul also points out that Jesus was of the tribe of Judah which was not connected with the Old Covenant priesthood.

[25] Ps 110:4; Heb 6:17; 7:21, 28.

Melchizedek offered his sacrifice on behalf of Abram, Jesus would offer His sacrifice on behalf of Abram/Abraham's offspring, those who are members of His Church.[26]

Some Protestants contend that Melchizedek's bread and wine offering was not a sacrifice and, therefore, Jesus' bread and wine offering at the Last Supper could not be a sacrifice. This is a rather naïve argument. After recording that Melchizedek offered bread and wine, Moses immediately writes "he was a priest of God Most High" (Gen 14:18). Moses conspicuously connects Melchizedek's *offering* of bread and wine to his priesthood because the duty of any priest is to "*offer* sacrifices" to God.[27]

Further, it would have been unnecessary for Melchizedek to bring out bread and wine solely for the soldiers' refreshment, for they were already well supplied with provisions from the booty they had taken in battle (Gen 14:11,16). The fact that the Genesis account records the offering but not the consumption of the bread and wine further underscores that the offering was first and foremost a priestly sacrifice. Even if the bread and wine were consumed by the assembly (which is almost certainly what occurred), this pattern of offering and eating followed the pattern of the Levitical sacrifices.

That Melchizedek is called a priest but didn't offer a blood sacrifice (or die on a cross) also demonstrates that his bread and wine offering was a sacrifice. This further demonstrates that Christ's offering of bread and wine at the Last Supper was a sacrifice, since Jesus' priesthood is patterned in the same manner as Melchizedek's. Further, because Scripture says Jesus made a "single sacrifice"[28] and a "single offering,"[29] this means that the Last Supper sacrifice and the sacrifice of the Cross are the *same sacrifice*.

---

[26] See, for example, Rom 4:16; Gal 3:29.
[27] See, for example, Heb 5:1, 3; 8:3.
[28] Heb 10:12.
[29] Heb 10:14.

We see the pattern of the Catholic Mass in Melchizedek's offering. Melchizedek offers bread and wine and calls upon God to bless Abram and the assembly. In return, Abram gives Melchizedek a tenth of everything. As we just mentioned, we can assume that those present consumed the bread and wine after it was offered to God in thanksgiving. This pattern follows the celebration of the Mass, where the priest offers the sacrifice, the sacrifice is consumed by the priest and the assembly, and the assembly in the offertory makes financial contributions to the Church so that she might serve the needs of the people. The difference, of course, as we will further examine in detail, is that the New Testament priests change the bread and wine into the Body and Blood of Christ.

We also note the relationship between Melchizedek and Abram. Even though Abram is one of the most righteous and faithful men in Scripture, he is inferior to Melchizedek. Melchizedek intercedes before God on Abram's behalf, and calls down God's blessings upon Abram. Abram then gives Melchizedek a percentage of the booty. In reference to Melchizedek, Paul says, "See how great he is! Abraham the patriarch gave him a tithe of the spoils . . . It is beyond dispute that the inferior is blessed by the superior" (Heb 7:4, 7). This underscores the dignity and sacredness of the priesthood. If Melchizedek, who ministered bread and wine, was viewed as superior to Abraham, how much more dignity must we accord to the priests who minister Christ's Body and Blood.[30]

---

[30] We mentioned how David prophesied about Christ's priesthood being modeled after that of Melchizedek. In the second book of Samuel, we read about how David made a similar offering of his own. While in Jerusalem, David brought forth the Ark of the Covenant, which contained the bread from heaven (6:12). Although David was a king, he vested himself in a priestly tunic and performed a liturgical dance before the Ark (v. 14). Then David offered sacrifices to God and blessed the people in the name of the Lord (v. 17-18). Thereafter, David distributed a portion of bread and wine to the assembly (v. 19). Sound familiar?

Because non-Catholics do not believe Jesus continues to offer His sacrifice in heaven, they want to limit Jesus' fulfillment of Melchizedek's priesthood to His actions at the Last Supper, where Jesus offered bread and wine. The problem with their view is that when Paul in his letter to the Hebrews describes Jesus' priesthood as after the order of Melchizedek, *it is always in the context of Jesus' perpetual priesthood in heaven*. Paul *never* mentions the Last Supper.

In fact, Paul negates the Protestant argument which seeks to limit Jesus' priesthood to His earthly sacrifice by emphatically stating, "Now if he [Jesus] were on earth, he would not be a priest at all, since there are priests who offer gifts according to the law" (Heb 8:4). Paul is clear that he is writing about Jesus' *heavenly* priesthood, which is the focus of the letter to the Hebrews.

We also note that Paul repeatedly says Jesus' priesthood is *forever* in the same manner as Melchizedek's priesthood.[31] This fulfills the prophecy in Psalm 110:4. If Jesus is no longer offering a bread and wine sacrifice in heaven, then describing Jesus' current priesthood as *forever* in the likeness of Melchizedek makes no sense. We would say only that Jesus' Last Supper offering was in the same manner as Melchizedek, *but not His current priesthood in heaven*.

We will first examine the biblical verses which demonstrate that Jesus is mysteriously offering His once-for-all sacrifice to the Father in heaven. In the next section, we will examine the words Jesus chose to institute the Eucharistic sacrifice and demonstrate how the Holy Mass makes present Jesus' eternal sacrifice.

THE PERPETUAL PRIESTHOOD OF JESUS CHRIST

The following verses from the book of Hebrews describe Jesus as our High Priest in heaven:

---

[31] Heb 5:6,10; 6:20; 7:15, 17.

- Since then we have a great high priest who has passed through the heavens, Jesus, the Son of God, let us hold fast our confession (Heb 4:14).
- . . . we have such a high priest, one who is seated at the right hand of the throne of the Majesty in heaven, a minister in the sanctuary and true tent which is set up not by man but by the Lord (Heb 8:1-2).
- But when Christ appeared as a high priest of the good things that have come . . . he entered once for all into the Holy Place . . ." (Heb 9:11-12).
- . . . since we have a great priest over the house of God, let us draw near with a true heart in full assurance of faith . . .[32]

Scripture teaches us that the principal duty of a priest is to *offer sacrifice*. Paul in the epistle to the Hebrews says, "for every high priest . . . is appointed to act on behalf of men in relation to God, to offer gifts and sacrifices for sins" (Heb 5:1). Paul further says, "For every high priest is appointed to offer gifts and sacrifices" (Heb 8:3). Paul then says about Jesus, in the very same verse, "hence it is necessary for this priest *also to have something to offer*."

To our non-Catholic friends, we must emphasize the following: Even though Jesus offered His Body once-for-all on the Cross of Calvary, Paul says it is necessary for Jesus to also have "something to offer" in heaven. Because Jesus is our High Priest in heaven, this necessary offering must be a "sacrifice for sins," for, according to Paul, that is what priests offer. We cannot separate Christ's sacrifice from His priesthood since Christ is a priest only by virtue of His sacrifice. That Scripture says Jesus must offer a sacrifice for sins in heaven poses an immediate problem for Protestant theology, which views Jesus' atoning work on the Cross as completed.

---

[32] Heb 10:21-22. See also Heb 2:17; 3:1.

What sacrifice for sins could Jesus be possibly offering in heaven? It could *only* be the sacrifice of His Body and Blood which He offered on the Cross and now makes present in heaven. This makes sense, for if the Father willed to be appeased only by the sacrifice of the Cross while Jesus was on earth, it follows that the Father would have to be appeased by this same sacrifice while Jesus is in heaven. If not, then the Father would now be willing to be appeased by something other than Christ's sacrifice (in fact, by something *less* than Christ's sacrifice). This is impossible because it would contravene God's perfect and immutable will which was "to bruise him . . . and be satisfied" (Is 53:10-11).

Why does God desire to be continually appeased? It is because we continually sin. As we have seen, God freely interacts with and responds to human freewill decisions, even though God resides in eternity. God chose to bind Himself to our time and space when He created us, and most especially when He redeemed us. Because God continues to be angered by sin, He demands an ongoing propitiation to forgive us of that sin. He required a continuous propitiation in the Old Covenant (with repeated animal sacrifices), and has willed the same in the New Covenant (with the repeated re-presentation of Christ's single sacrifice). We will further examine the ongoing process of propitiation and forgiveness later in the book.

Jesus' "Once for All" Sacrifice

While Jesus makes present His eternal sacrifice in heaven, we must point out that He no longer suffers. Jesus is not being sacrificed over and over again in heaven or in the Mass. Jesus presents to the Father the sacrifice that He offered "once for all" — that is, "once" for "all" people, places, and times. This is not a new sacrifice, but the *same* sacrifice. Jesus shows His Father the work He was sent to do. In attempting to grasp this mystery, it is extremely important to understand the following truth: *Scripture distinguishes between Christ's past suffering and death and the current re-presentation of His sacrifice in heaven.*

This is why the Scriptures always describe Jesus' sufferings in the past tense. For example, Paul says, "For because he himself has suffered and been tempted, he is able to help those who are tempted" (Heb 2:18); "Although he was a Son, he learned obedience through what he suffered" (Heb 5:8); "So Jesus also suffered outside the gate in order to sanctify the people through his own blood" (Heb 13:12). The book of 1 Peter also says "because Christ also suffered for you,"[33] and "Christ suffered in the flesh" (1 Pet 4:1).

However, when Scripture speaks of Christ's sacrifice, it never relegates it to the past. Instead, Scripture connects Christ's *sacrifice* with His *appearance* in heaven to emphasize that *both the sacrifice and the appearance are ongoing.* For example, in describing Christ's sacrifice, Paul says, ". . . he did this *once for all* when he offered up himself" (Heb 7:27).[34] Paul uses the same phrase to describe Jesus' appearance in heaven: ". . . he entered *once for all* into the Holy Place, taking not the blood of goats and calves but his own blood, thus securing an eternal redemption" (Heb 9:12).

In both Hebrews 7:27 and 9:12, Paul is distinguishing the Old Covenant priesthood from Jesus' priesthood. The Old Covenant priests had to go in and out of the Holy Place every year to offer their sacrifices to God.[35] In the New Covenant, Jesus *also* enters into the Holy Place to offer His sacrifice, but He does so once for all, there to stay, and never to leave again. Neither Jesus' sacrifice nor His entrance into the Holy Place has to be repeated. Instead, both Jesus' sacrifice and His entrance into

---

[33] 1 Pet 2:21; see also 1 Pet 2:23.
[34] See also Heb 10:10; 1 Pet 3:18.
[35] See Heb 9:6-7, 25.

heaven *are perpetual.* This is what Paul means when he uses the phrase "once for all."[36]

Scripture provides additional insights into the eternal nature of Christ's sacrifice. For example, in the context of Jesus' heavenly priesthood and ongoing intercession before the Father, Paul says that Jesus' "works were finished from the foundation of the world."[37] In the Apocalypse, which also describes Jesus' heavenly reign, John refers to Jesus as "the Lamb which was slain from the beginning of the world."[38]

Both Paul and John emphasize that there is an *eternal* dimension to Christ's sacrifice in His role as High Priest. The Father views Jesus as the slain Lamb from all eternity, and for all eternity. Paul makes this clear when he says that Jesus "holds his priesthood permanently, because he continues forever"[39] and that "Jesus Christ is the same yesterday, today and forever."[40]

This is why God could dispense His grace in the Old Covenant. As we alluded to, in the Old Covenant, God could for-

---

[36] This conclusion is necessary if we are to maintain exegetical consistency between Heb 7:27 and 9:12. Both verses deal with entering into the Holy Place to offer sacrifice, but distinguish between the Old Covenant method and the New Covenant method. In the Old Covenant, the priests would have to repeat both their entrance into the Holy Place and the sacrifice they offered. In the New Covenant, there is only once entrance into the Holy Place and one sacrifice offered. Because the appearance of the Priest in the Holy Place is perpetual, then the sacrifice must be perpetual as well. *This is because the purpose of entering the Holy Place is to offer the sacrifice.*

[37] Heb 4:3. See also 1 Pet 1:20, where Peter similarly says Christ "was destined before the foundation of the world." Peter makes this statement in the context of the Eucharist, right after he describes "the precious blood of Christ, like that of a lamb without blemish or spot" (v. 19), and before he describes the Church as "a holy priesthood, to offer spiritual sacrifices acceptable to God through Jesus Christ" (2:5).

[38] Apoc 13:8 (DR). See also Heb 13:20, where Paul uses the word "eternal" to describe the blood of the covenant.

[39] Heb 7:24.

[40] Heb 13:8. Paul makes this statement between his description of the Eucharistic liturgy in Heb 11:22-25 and Heb 13:10-16.

give sin because He foresaw Christ's anticipated bloodshed. In the New Covenant, God forgives our sin because He is satisfied by Christ's actual bloodshed. With the implementation of the New Covenant, God no longer requires to see the shed blood of animals in the Temple because He now sees the shed blood of His Son. This, as we will further develop below, occurs in the Temple of heaven and on earth, in the Holy Mass. Christ's sacrifice is eternal because it extends backward and forward throughout time and space.

"It Is Finished"

Many Protestants who acknowledge that Christ's death was a propitiatory sacrifice often point to Jesus' utterance "It is finished" while on the Cross to prove that His propitiation was completed at Calvary (Jn 19:30). If true, then there is no need for Christ to continue to propitiate the Father in heaven or through the Holy Mass. However, there are a number of problems with this Protestant argument.

First, since Jesus' works were "finished" from the foundation of the world, Scripture gives the word "finished" a relative meaning. If Jesus' works were literally finished from "the foundation of the world," then there would have been no need for Him to become Incarnate and die on a cross for our sins. We see the relative nature of the word "finished" in Jn 17:4, where Jesus says that He has "finished" the work that the Father sent Him to do.[41] However, at this point, Jesus had not yet gone to the Cross, so His work was not really "finished."

Scripture's use of "finished" is similar to its use of "once for all." Scripture shows that on the one hand, Christ's death was "once for all"; but, on other hand, His death is connected to His "once for all" appearance in heaven. Similarly, on the one hand, Christ's death "finished" that part of His work; but, on the other

---

[41] John uses almost identical words for the verb "finish" in Jn 17:4 (*teleio*) and Jn 19:30 (*teleo*).

hand, Christ can "finish" His work after His death in another mode. Nothing precludes Christ's "once for all" death from being re-presented in heaven and in the Mass.

Second, Scripture shows that Jesus' work is *not* finished, even after His death. As we will further examine below, through His eternal priesthood, Jesus continues to "work" by interceding before the Father on our behalf for our salvation.[42] In fact, Jesus' work will not be "finished" until His Second Coming, when He will bring to completion the New Covenant and place all His enemies under His feet.[43]

Third, from a lexical and exegetical perspective, one cannot conclude that the phrase "It is finished" refers to Christ's saving work or His propitiation of the Father. The word for "finished" (from the Greek *teleo*) in Jn 19:30 has no subject, which means it is unclear what the "it" refers to. This is why the translation reads "*It* is finished." However, because the same Greek word is used in the second preceding verse (Jn 19:28) *and* vv. 28 and 30 are connected contextually, Jn 19:28's use of "finished" helps us understand its meaning in Jn 19:30.

In Jn 19:28, we read:

> After this Jesus, knowing that all was now finished, said (*to fulfill the scripture*), "I thirst."

In this verse, the Apostle John makes it clear that the word "finished" refers to Christ's *fulfillment of the Scripture*. This "fulfillment of Scripture" in v. 28 is the only contextual referent we have for the phrase "It is finished" in v. 30. Thus, at most, Jesus was saying that the Scriptural prophecies of His suffering and death had now come to pass. However, Jn 19:30 does not prevent the work Jesus does *after* His suffering and death from continuing in another form.

---

[42] Heb 7:25; Rom 8:32-34.
[43] See Heb 10:13; Ps 110:1.

What did Jesus really mean when He said "I thirst"? He was thirsting to satisfy the Father's wrath against our sins. The wine Jesus receives is an allusion to the cup of God's wrath.[44] Jesus presents the cup at the Last Supper,[45] acknowledges it in the Garden of Gethsemane,[46] refuses to drink it while He carries His cross,[47] until He finally completes His propitiatory sacrifice (Jn 19:30). This continuity of the "cup" from the Last Supper to the Cross underscores that they are *one and the same sacrifice.* Psalm 116 also connects the "cup of salvation" (v. 13) with the "sacrifice of thanksgiving" (v. 17). This also links the cup on Good Friday with the Eucharistic sacrifice.

JESUS OFFERS HIS BLOOD SACRIFICE IN HEAVEN

The manner in which Christ presents His blood sacrifice to the Father in heaven is a mystery. Yet the book of Hebrews sheds light on the reality of this mystery. As we have seen, Paul says that Jesus "entered once for all into the Holy Place, *taking* not the blood of goats and calves *but his own blood,* thus securing an eternal redemption" (Heb 9:12). Why does Paul emphasize that Jesus takes His blood into heaven? To emphasize that Jesus' blood is being presented in heaven *as a sacrifice.*

Paul does this by setting up a comparison between the Old Testament priests, who sacrificed animals, and Jesus Christ, who sacrificed Himself. Just as the Old Testament priests would take the blood of these animals into the earthly sanctuary, Jesus takes His Blood into the "heavenly sanctuary."[48] Further, just as God would see the shed blood of the animals and be temporarily appeased, He now sees the shed blood of His Son and is perfectly

---

[44] Is 51:17, 22; Jer 25:15; Apoc 19:15.
[45] Mt 26:27; Mk 14:23; 22:20.
[46] Mt 26:39; Mk 14:36; Lk 22:42; Jn 18:11.
[47] Mt 27:34; Mk 15:23.
[48] See Heb 8:2; 9:12; 10:19.

appeased. To maintain parity between Paul's explanations of the Old Covenant versus New Covenant sacrificial system, we must conclude that *both* the animal blood on earth and Jesus' blood in heaven are being described in the context of sacrifice.[49]

Paul supports this conclusion in the next two verses when he says:

> For if the sprinkling of defiled persons with the blood of goats and bulls and with the ashes of a heifer sanctifies for the purification of the flesh, how much more shall the blood of Christ, who through the eternal Spirit offered himself without blemish to God, purify your conscience from dead works to serve the living God.[50]

Again, we look at these verses in context.

Paul describes how the blood of animals was sprinkled in sacrifice on the people in the Old Covenant, and how the blood of Christ is likewise applied to the people of the New Covenant. Specifically, Paul is describing the *ongoing* application of Christ's *ongoing* blood sacrifice in heaven which purifies the consciences of believers. This purification is described in the *present tense* because Christ's blood *presently offered* is bringing about the purification.[51]

---

[49] Some Protestants argue that since the Old Covenant priests did not take the victim into the earthly sanctuary, Christ is only a priest, but not a victim, in the heavenly sanctuary. The Catholic rejoinder: First, since the Old Covenant priest was not also the victim (but Christ is both), the typology does not demand a one-to-one correspondence. Second, in order for Christ to be a priest in heaven, He, according to Paul's letter to the Hebrews, must be offering a sacrifice (which is the immolation of Himself). Third, the Old Covenant priest did bring the blood of the victim into the earthly sanctuary, and that is why Paul focuses on the presence of Christ's blood in the heavenly sanctuary when compared to the Old Covenant system.

[50] Heb 9:13-14. The purification, or cleansing (from the Greek *katharizo*), is occurring in the present tense.

[51] See also Heb 7:25; 8:6; 10:19, 29; 12:24; and 13:21, which connect the ongoing priestly work of Christ with its ongoing effects.

Through the perpetual offering of Christ's blood in heaven, the Father is propitiated, our sins are expiated, and we can "serve the living God" with a pure conscience. This is something that the Old Covenant sacrifices could not do (see Heb 9:9).

The New Covenant "Sacrifices"

Paul makes an even more dramatic comparison between the Old Covenant sacrifices and Jesus' heavenly sacrifice in the next few verses. Paul describes how Moses ratified the first covenant by sprinkling the people and the liturgical elements with the blood of the animals[52] while saying, "This is the blood of the covenant which God commanded you" (Heb 9:20). (It is no surprise that Jesus used the same words when He offered His Blood in sacrifice at the Last Supper, which we will address later.)

Then Paul writes something that should be striking to our non-Catholic friends. He compares the Old Covenant sacrifices with the sacrifice of Christ by referring to the New Covenant sacrifice as "sacrifices," *in the plural form*. He says:

> Indeed, under the law almost everything is purified with blood, and without the shedding of blood there is no forgiveness of sins. Thus it was necessary for the copies of the heavenly things to be purified with these rites, but the heavenly things themselves *with better sacrifices than these*. For Christ has entered, not into a sanctuary made with hands, a copy of the true one, but into heaven itself, now to appear in the presence of God on our behalf.
>
> — HEB 9:22-24 [53]

Let's examine these verses. Because God willed to forgive our sins through bloodshed, Paul explains that both the Old and

---

[52] Heb 9:18-19, 21.

[53] There are no textual variants for the word "sacrifices" in the Greek manuscripts; thus, Protestants cannot deny that Paul refers to New Covenant "sacrifices," in the plural.

New Covenants have a "shedding of blood" requirement. Paul first describes the rite of purification with blood under the Old Covenant (v. 22), and then the same blood purification rite in the New Covenant (v. 23). In connection with this shedding of blood, Paul says that those in the New Covenant are purified with better *sacrifices* than those in the Old Covenant.[54]

There is only *one* New Covenant blood sacrifice which purifies us and forgives our sins. That is the sacrifice of Jesus on Calvary. Therefore, Paul reveals that Christ's Calvary sacrifice has a plural dimension to it. As we will further develop, this plural dimension of Christ's sacrifice is fulfilled *only in the context of its sacramental re-presentation in heaven and on earth in the Holy Mass*. This is the pure, single sacrifice that is continually offered from sunrise to sunset, around the world, in the Eucharist (as was prophesied by Jeremiah and Malachi).

Paul makes this connection between Christ's sacrifice in heaven and the Eucharistic sacrifice on earth in a number of verses in his letter to the Hebrews. Before Paul reveals Christ's "sacrifices" in heaven, he says that Jesus "is the mediator of a new covenant" (Heb 9:15). In the context of Jesus' mediation of the covenant, Paul describes how Jesus takes His Blood into heaven to forgive sin. The only time Jesus uses the phrase "New Covenant" is when He instituted the Eucharist. Jesus said, "This cup is the new covenant in my blood,"[55] and "This is the blood of the covenant which is poured out for many for the forgiveness of sins."[56] The terms *new covenant, blood,* and *forgiveness of sin* in

---

[54] The "copies of the heavenly things" in v. 23 refer to the people of the Old Covenant, as well as the tent, the book, and the liturgical vessels that they used. The "heavenly things" in the same verse refer to the people of the New Covenant, the citizens of heaven (Eph 2:19). The focus in both usages is the "people," since the "shedding of blood" is for the forgiveness of the people's sins.

[55] Lk 22:20; 1 Cor 11:25. See also Mt 26:28; Mk 14:24; Heb 9:20.

[56] Mt 26:28; Mk 14:24. See also Lk 22:20; 1 Cor 11:25; Heb 9:20.

Heb 9 appear together in Scripture in only one other place: *in the accounts of Jesus instituting the Holy Eucharist.*

This connects the "sacrifices" of Hebrews with the Eucharistic sacrifice of the Gospels. That connection, along with the fact that Christ's heavenly priesthood is modeled after that of Melchizedek, who offered bread and wine, makes it clear that the "sacrifices" occurring in the heavenly sanctuary are the same "sacrifices" occurring in the Holy Mass. When He commanded His apostles at the Last Supper to "do this in memory of me," Jesus mandated that these "sacrifices" occur on earth in the Mass.[57] The "sacrifices" of Heb 9:23 refer to the one sacrifice of the Mass, offered in a plurality of locations through the world, as revealed in Mal 1:11.

Protestants often point to Paul's subsequent teaching in Heb 9:26 where he says that Jesus "has appeared once for all at the end of the age to put away sin by the sacrifice of himself." Because Paul refers to Jesus' sacrifice in v. 26 in the singular, they argue that this somehow negates Paul's use of "sacrifices" in the plural in v. 23. This implies that Paul made a mistake in v. 23, and then corrected the mistake in v. 26. Of course, such exegesis calls into question the process of divine inspiration and the integrity of the whole Bible. In short, it accuses God, the author of Scripture, of inspiring error. This is no way to exegete Sacred Scripture.

From a Catholic perspective, Paul's descriptions of Christ's sacrifice in both the singular and the plural make perfect sense. They reveal both sides of the same coin. Christ's single "sacrifice" in v. 26 is described as "sacrifices" in v. 23 in the context of its repeated application to sinners throughout time and space in the Holy Mass. There is absolutely no exegetical basis to drive a wedge between the single sacrifice of v. 26 and the plural sacrifices of v. 23, since both are describing the eternal sacrifice of Christ, offered in the same manner as Melchizedek, under the administration of the New Covenant.

---

[57] See Lk 22:19; 1 Cor 11:24-25.

The Lamb Slain before the Throne in Heaven

Because Jesus presents His blood sacrifice to the Father in heaven, it is no surprise that John refers to Jesus as the "Lamb" in the Apocalypse. In fact, John calls Jesus the Lamb twenty-eight times in this letter, and it is always in the context of Jesus' sacerdotal functions in heaven.[58] The Apocalypse is full of revelations that John received concerning what is currently happening in heaven, as well as what will happen before the end times.

Of course, describing Jesus as a Lamb emphasizes His propitiatory death, which takes away our sins. John the Baptist said of Jesus, "Behold, the Lamb of God, who takes away the sin of the world!"[59] Peter says that we were ransomed "with the precious blood of Christ, like that of a lamb without blemish or spot" (1 Pet 1:19). Isaiah prophesied that Jesus would be led to the slaughter "like a lamb before its shearer."[60] Now, in the Apocalypse, John uses the same terminology to describe what he actually sees: *Jesus appears in heaven as a sacrificed Lamb.*

We see John's first use of this description in Apoc 5:6:

> And between the throne and the four living creatures and among the elders, I saw a *Lamb standing, as though it had been slain.*

There are a number of interesting facts about John's vision. First, we see Jesus *standing* in His slain condition. Lambs that are slain do not stand. This underscores that Jesus is actively presenting His slain condition in the heaven sanctuary.[61]

---

[58] Apoc 5:6, 8, 12-13; 6:1, 16; 7:9-10, 14, 17; 8:1; 12:11; 13:8, 11; 14:1, 4, 10; 15:3; 17:14; 19:7, 9; 21:9, 14, 22-23, 27; 22:1, 3.

[59] Jn 1:29; see also Jn 1:36.

[60] Is 53:7; see also Acts 8:32.

[61] That Jesus opens the seals of God's judgment also demonstrates His active priesthood in heaven (Apoc 5:1-2, 5, 9; 6:1, 3, 5, 7, 9, 12; 8:1).

The Greek is translated as "having been standing" (*histemi*) and "having been slain" (*sphazo*). John's use of perfect participles to describe both Christ's standing and slain conditions indicate that Christ began to exhibit these conditions at a specific moment in the past, and that both conditions *are ongoing*. John's description of Jesus standing in heaven follows that of Stephen who "gazed into heaven and saw the glory of God, and Jesus *standing* at the right hand of God."[62]

We also note that Jesus stands as a slain Lamb *before the throne*. This is similar to Paul's descriptions of Jesus in the heavenly sanctuary. In fact, both Paul and John depict the throne as the place where God the Father is seated.[63] John elsewhere distinguishes between the Lamb and the throne to emphasize what Jesus is doing in heaven: He appears *before* the throne of God *to present His slain condition to the Father.*[64]

In the context of Jesus' appearance as a slain Lamb, John also refers to the altar in heaven.[65] This alludes to the book of Hebrews' use of "altar" to describe the heavenly liturgy and also puts Jesus' appearance before the Father in the context of sacrifice (Heb 13:10). There would be no altar in heaven unless a sacrifice was being offered. John also sees the prayers of the saints rising to the Father as incense before the heavenly altar, and the souls of the martyrs underneath the altar.[66] These prayers are united to the sacrifice of Christ, and both are presented to the Father.

---

[62] Acts 7:55; see also Acts 7:56.

[63] Heb 1:8; 4:16; 8:1; 12:2; Apoc 1:4; 3:21; 4:2-6, 9-10; 5:1, 6-7, 11, 13; 6:16; 7:9-11, 15, 17; 8:3; 12:5; 14:3; 16:17; 19:4-5; 20:11-12; 21:3, 5; 22:1-3.

[64] See, for example, Apoc 3:21; 5:13; 6:16; 7:10; and 22:1, 3, where John distinguishes between the position of the Lamb and the throne before which the Lamb appears.

[65] Apoc 6:9; 8:3, 5; 9:13; 11:1; 14:18; 16:7.

[66] See Apoc 5:8; 6:9; 8:3-5. See also Apoc 9:13; 11:1; 14:18; 16:7.

John further sees Jesus clothed with a long robe and golden girdle (Apoc 1:13). These were the same vestments worn by the Levitical priests who offered animal sacrifices (see Ex 28:4). John further describes Jesus as "clad in a robe dipped in blood" (Apoc 19:13). This is another striking description of Jesus' slain condition, and underscores the presence of Jesus' blood sacrifice in heaven. John also connects Jesus' slain condition to its propitiatory effects on the Father as he then says, "He will tread the wine press of the fury of the wrath of God the Almighty" (Apoc 19:15).

John also writes about those who "have washed their robes and made them white in the blood of the Lamb" (Apoc 7:14). These are the ones who are "before the throne of God, and serve him day and night within his temple" (Apoc 7:15). Again, John connects Christ's shed blood with the "throne of God" and the "temple," terminology that Paul uses in the book of Hebrews as he describes Jesus' heavenly priesthood. In this vision, Jesus is including these saints in the presentation of His blood sacrifice "before the throne" and in the heavenly "temple." Through Christ's ongoing offering, these people were able to defeat the devil "by the blood of the Lamb."[67] These graphic descriptions underscore the ongoing presence and effects of Christ's shed blood in heaven.

Jesus connects His heavenly priesthood to the Eucharist in the Apocalypse when He says, "To him who conquers I will give some of the hidden manna" (Apoc 2:17). The manna of the Old Covenant was the bread from heaven with which God fed Israel during its journey to the Promised Land. It foreshadowed the true bread from heaven which God gives to His Church during its journey to the Promised Land of heaven. The manna is "hidden" by our senses but revealed by faith, which God desires from His New Covenant people.

Thus, as our eternal High Priest, Jesus invites us through the Eucharist into full covenant communion with God:

---

[67] Apoc 12:11; see also Apoc 1:5; 5:9.

"Behold, I stand at the door and knock; if any one hears my voice and opens the door, I will come in to him and eat with him, and he with me."

— Apoc 3:20

Because those in heaven are already in eternal communion with God, Jesus is talking about giving His heavenly manna to those *on earth*. This happens in the celebration of the Eucharist in the Holy Mass: "Blessed are those who are invited to the marriage supper of the Lamb" (Apoc 19:9).

The Blood of the New Covenant

Paul also uses the particular phrase "blood of the covenant" in his letter to the Hebrews. For example, after describing the heavenly liturgy and the earthly priesthood,[68] Paul says:

May the God of peace . . . by the *blood of the eternal covenant*, equip you with everything good that you may do his will.

— Heb 13:20-21

For those who refuse to "meet together"[69] to celebrate the Eucharist, Paul says such people have "spurned the Son of God, and profaned the *blood of the covenant* by which he was sanctified."[70]

Why is this significant? Because the New Testament uses the phrase "blood of the covenant" only one other time: *when Jesus*

---

[68] After Paul explains that we actually participate in the heavenly liturgy by coming to Christ's sprinkled blood (12:24), eating from the heavenly altar (13:5), and offering up the continual sacrifice of praise (13:10), Paul exhorts us to "obey your leaders and submit to them; for they are keeping watch over your souls as men who will have to give account" (13:17).

[69] Heb 10:25.

[70] Heb 10:29. This verse also proves that true Christians can fall away from the faith. These people who "profaned the blood of the covenant" had already been "sanctified" by the Eucharist. This is contrary to the Protestant idea that sanctification occurs in a person who is eternally secure.

instituted the Eucharist (see Mt 26:28). Paul may have used the phrase "blood of the covenant" because he received instruction on the Eucharist directly from Jesus Himself (see 1 Cor 11:23). Because in the book of Hebrews, Paul is speaking of the *actual* shed blood of Christ (for only Christ's true blood can "equip" us to do God's will, and be "profaned" if we refuse Him), then it necessarily follows that Christ's *actual* shed blood is also present in the Eucharist (which is what the people celebrated by "meeting together"). If not, then Paul would be guilty of a gross misapplication of Christ's words.

The Mediator of the New Covenant

Paul also connects Jesus' role as "mediator" with the words "blood" and "covenant." For example, after Paul states how the blood of Christ purifies our consciences to serve the living God,[71] in the next verse he says:

> Therefore he is the mediator of a new covenant, so that those who are called may receive the promised eternal inheritance.
>
> — HEB 9:15

Paul also tells us that we have come "to Jesus, the mediator of a new covenant, and to the sprinkled blood that speaks more graciously than the blood of Abel."[72] Paul further says:

> Christ has obtained a ministry which is as much more excellent than the old as the covenant he mediates is better, since it is enacted on better promises.[73]

---

[71] Heb 9:14.

[72] Heb 12:24. Paul also says that "there is one *mediator* between God and men, the man Christ Jesus, who *gave himself* as a ransom for all (1 Tim 2:5-6). As in the book of Hebrews, Paul connects Jesus' mediation with His sacrifice.

[73] Heb 8:6. The Greek word for "ministry" is *leitourgos*, from which the Church gets the word "liturgy" to describe the celebration of the Mass.

These verses demonstrate that Jesus did not just establish the New Covenant in His blood; *He mediates it as well.*[74] What does this mean? Mediation is the process by which one intervenes between conflicting parties to promote reconciliation. According to Paul, Jesus mediates on our behalf in reconciling us to God *by presenting His shed blood to the Father.*

For example, Paul says that Jesus' sprinkled blood *speaks* to God more graciously than that of Abel (Heb 12:24). This "speaking" of Jesus' blood occurs in "the city of the living God, the heavenly Jerusalem," and in the presence of "innumerable angels in festal gathering, and to the assembly of the first-born who are enrolled in heaven, and to a judge who is God of all, and to the spirits of just men made perfect" (Heb 12:22-23). In His mediatorial role, Jesus' sprinkled blood appears in heaven and speaks to God on our behalf.

Paul refers to Abel's blood to emphasize that the shedding of innocent blood merits the Father's pity. When Cain killed Abel, God told Cain "the voice of your brother's blood *is crying to me from the ground*" (Gen 4:10). Notice that Abel's blood appeared to God in an earthly sanctuary, where Abel had been offering propitiatory sacrifices to God.[75] Notice also that, even though Abel died once, the presence of his shed blood had an ongoing effect on God (God says the blood *is crying* rather than *has cried*).

The presence of Christ's blood in the heavenly sanctuary also has a continual effect on God. Although shed only once, it continually speaks to God even more graciously than the blood of Abel because it appeases the Father more than any other sacrifice ever could. Right after Paul says, "Christ's blood *speaks*

---

[74] Notice again that while Jesus' suffering is described in the past tense, Jesus' mediation is always described in the present tense.

[75] Gen 4:2-4.

more graciously," he subtly warns us in the next verse: "See that you do not refuse him *who is speaking*" (Heb 12:25). Paul's use of the present tense is another indication that the pleading of Christ's blood in heaven is *occurring at the present time.*

Our non-Catholic friends often point to 1 Timothy 2:5 when criticizing prayers to the saints.[76] This passage says, "There is one mediator between God and men, the man Christ Jesus . . ." While it is true that Jesus is our one mediator, we must explain *how* Jesus accomplishes that mediation. As we have seen, it is through the presentation of His shed blood in heaven. This is why Paul connects Jesus' *mediation* with His *sacrifice* in the next verse: ". . . who *gave himself* as a ransom for all" (v. 6).

JESUS' ONGOING MEDIATION FOR OUR SALVATION

We now explore in more depth the purpose of Jesus' perpetual sacrifice in heaven: *to save us from sin and eternal damnation.*

Because we constantly struggle with sin, we need Christ's constant, propitiatory mediation. God responds to this mediation by forgiving our sins and granting us the effectual graces necessary to persevere in faith to the end of our lives. Paul says:

> Consequently he is able for all time *to save those* who draw near to God through him, since he always lives to make *intercession* for them.
>
> — HEB 7:25

The phrase "to make intercession" is from the Greek *entugchano*, which is a present tense verb that literally means "to be pleading." Paul is clear that our salvation depends upon Christ's *ongoing* pleading with the Father.

---

[76] See my book *The Biblical Basis for the Catholic Faith*, pp. 143-156, for a thorough refutation of the Protestant arguments against prayers to the saints.

To the Romans, Paul also says:

He who did not spare his own Son but *gave him up* for us all, will he not also give us all things with him? Who shall bring any charge against God's elect? It is God who *justifies*; who is to condemn? Is it Christ Jesus, who died, yes, who was raised from the dead, who is at the right hand of God, who indeed *intercedes* for us?

— ROM 8:32-34

Once again, we see Jesus currently interceding for us for the purpose of justifying us (vv 33-34). "Justifies" is another word for "saves," which is set in opposition to the word "condemn" (v. 34).[77] Paul uses the same word for "intercedes" that he used in Heb 7:25. Moreover, Christ's justifying intercession occurs in the context of having given Himself up in sacrifice (vv. 32, 34).

Of course, the ultimate reason for Christ's heavenly intercession is because *He loves us.* He pleads our case before the Father so that we will be granted the grace to avoid sin and ultimately live with Him forever. Because "God is love,"[78] and to love is to sacrifice, Christ's sacrifice is an eternal act of love. We might even say that "God is sacrifice," because He never stops loving us.

Christ's ongoing intercession to save us from sin and death creates a significant problem for Protestant theology. In some forms of Evangelical Protestantism, once a person accepts Jesus as personal Lord and Savior, he is eternally saved. His sins are forever washed away and he cannot lose his salvation. If this is true,

---

[77] In Catholic theology, justification and salvation are synonymous terms because they both happen at the same time. See, for example, Jesus' statement in Mt 12:37: "For by your words you will be *justified*, and by your words you will be *condemned*." Justification (salvation) is the opposite of condemnation. Paul also uses the word "justified" instead of "saved" in Romans 8:30.

[78] See 1 Jn 4:8, 16.

however, then Christ does not need to continue to intercede for us to save us; we are already saved.

Protestants often respond that Christ intercedes for us to maintain God's promise that He will not deal with us the way He would have without Jesus. This rebuttal, of course, begs the question. If we are "once saved, always saved" by accepting Jesus as Lord and Savior, then there is nothing left for Jesus to do. If accepting the imputed righteousness of Christ is all that one needs to procure salvation, why isn't that one-time imputation enough?

Protestants also explain that Jesus intercedes before the Father to restore to "fellowship" those saved Christians who have fallen into sin. There are obvious problems with this rebuttal as well. The most obvious problem is that neither Heb 7:25 nor Rom 8:34 say anything about "fellowship." Instead, these verses expressly state that Jesus' intercession is *for the purpose of our salvation.*

Scripture also makes no distinction between being "out of fellowship" with God and being "condemned." If one falls from grace,[79] he is under the condemnation of the law and needs to be "reconciled to God."[80] This is what Jesus' ongoing intercession is able to do. Moreover, if the Christian is truly saved, then this makes Christ's intercession superfluous. He would not need to be "restored" at all, since his salvation would be guaranteed. This is another glaring contradiction in Protestant theology.

---

[79] Gal 5:4. Paul says the Galatians have fallen from grace even though they have received the Holy Spirit (3:2-3, 5) and are called "sons of God" (3:26; 4:6-7).

[80] 2 Cor 5:20. Paul exhorts the Corinthians to be reconciled to God, even though he says they stand firm in their faith (1:24), are being conformed to the glory of Christ (3:18; 4:16), and have the Holy Spirit (3:3). Paul views the reconciliation process as ongoing because Jesus' mediation is ongoing, and it is Jesus' mediation that is bringing about the reconciliation.

Jesus Is the Ongoing Propitiation for Our Sins

There are additional passages in Scripture which describe the reality and effects of Jesus' ongoing propitiation. For example, in the book of Hebrews, Paul says:

> Wherefore it behoved him in all things to be made like unto his brethren, that he might become a merciful and faithful priest before God, that he might be a *propitiation for the sins of the people.* For in that, wherein he himself hath suffered and been tempted, he is able to succour them also that are tempted.[81]

As with his letter to the Romans, Paul connects Jesus' heavenly priesthood with His being a propitiation for sin. Paul says that Jesus appears in heaven as a "priest before God" to be a "propitiation for the sins of the people" (v. 17). Paul does not limit Jesus' propitiatory sacrifice to the hill on Calvary, but sees it extending into heaven through His perpetual priesthood. This passage also reminds us of both Paul and John's imagery of Jesus appearing "before" the throne of God as a slain Lamb. Jesus is both priest and victim in the heavenly sanctuary — the one offering and being offered.

Because Jesus is an ongoing propitiation, Paul says that "he is able to help those who are tempted" (v. 18). This is the purpose and effect of Jesus' propitiation. Because Jesus appeases the Father's wrath through His heavenly sacrifice, the Father responds by granting grace and mercy to those who are being tempted. This coincides with Heb 7:25 and Rom 8:34, where Jesus' intercession is currently taking place in heaven to save those who have fallen. Jesus currently helps because we currently sin.

Paul further says to the Hebrews:

---

[81] Heb 2:17-18 (DR).

> Let us then with confidence draw near to the throne of
> grace, that we may receive mercy and find grace to help in
> time of need.
>
> — HEB 4:16

The "throne of grace" refers to the place where Jesus appears
before the Father as a slain Lamb. In our time of need (that is,
when we sin), Jesus' perpetual appearance before the Father
appeases His wrath against the sin, and we instead receive His
grace and mercy.

John also describes Jesus as an ongoing propitiation in
heaven. He says:

> My little children, these things I write to you, that you
> may not sin. But if any man sin, we have an advocate with
> the Father, Jesus Christ the just: And he is the *propitiation
> for our sins*: and not for ours only, but also for those of the
> whole world.[82]

Let us also examine this passage. First, in connection with
our forgiveness, we note that John refers to his readers as "little
children." While Protestants want to make the Atonement a
mere legal transaction (to avoid "propitiation" and the need for
the Mass), John's use of "little children" demonstrates that he
views it primarily as a familial, or covenantal, relationship. The
merits of Christ's sacrifice are not imputed by law to defendants
in a courtroom, but given by grace to the "children" of the New
Covenant.

Second, as in Heb 2:17, John connects Jesus' *advocacy* with
propitiation. Because Paul describes our having an advocate in the
present tense ("we have an advocate"), the advocacy and its effects
("he is the propitiation") are also occurring in the present. Jesus'

---

[82] 1 Jn 2:1-2 (DR). Notice that Jesus' propitiation is described in the present tense: "He is the propitiation" (*autos hilasmos eimi*).

ongoing advocacy (or "intercession" used in Heb 7:25 and Rom 8:34) brings about the forgiveness of sin by appeasing the Father's anger against that sin. Like Paul, John underscores the temporal relationship between us committing sin (on earth) and Jesus propitiating the Father to forgive our sin (in heaven).

Third, John says *if* we sin, *then* Jesus is the propitiation for those sins. John is not focusing on *all* sins, but only on *potential* sins, and says that Jesus is the current propitiation for those sins *if and when they occur.* John is connecting our potentiality to sin with Jesus' potentiality to propitiate the Father for that sin. Both potentialities exist at the *present time.* This demonstrates that Jesus propitiates the Father currently through the presentation of His once-for-all sacrifice. If we should sin, Jesus' ongoing propitiation in heaven is able to merit from the Father the forgiveness of the sin.

As an aside, many Protestant Bibles translate "propitiation" (Greek, *hilaskomai*) as "expiation." This demonstrates a bias toward the view that the Atonement is a legal transaction. *Propitiation* deals with appeasing the anger of the offended, whereas *expiation* deals with removing the sin from the offender. Protestants prefer to use *expiation* in describing the Atonement because it keeps the focus on what happens to the sinner. As such, it can accommodate the view of a legal or forensic imputation of Christ's righteousness which is applied to the sinner when he accepts the "payment." It also avoids having to explain how Jesus could be an ongoing propitiation in heaven and in the Mass.

The problem is that *expiation is the result of propitiation.* God will not expiate sin and infuse grace until He is propitiated. The propitiation must be personal (through Christ's sinless and voluntary offering) and not legal (in which case Christ would have suffered eternally and everyone would be guaranteed heaven). Moreover, Scripture demonstrates that *hilaskomai* and its derivatives are generally used to describe the process of appeasing wrath and averting anger, and thus *propitiation* is the proper translation.[83]

How Do We Benefit from Jesus' Ongoing Propitiation?

Our discussion about Jesus' ongoing propitiation raises the next logical question: *How* is Jesus' propitiation applied to the sinner so that his sins are forgiven? *How* do we benefit from Jesus' priestly intercession before the Father? John provides the answer:

> But if we walk in the light, as he is in the light, we have fellowship with one another, and the blood of Jesus his Son cleanses us from all sin. If we say we have no sin, we deceive ourselves, and the truth is not in us. *If we confess our sins*, he is faithful and just, and will forgive our sins and cleanse us from all unrighteousness.[84]

In order to receive the grace of forgiveness, John says *we must confess our sins*. If we confess our sins, then God *will* forgive them and cleanse us through the blood of His Son which is being offered by Jesus in the heavenly sanctuary. If we don't confess our sins, we do not benefit from Jesus' mediatorial propitiation. Instead, we remain under God's divine wrath and stand condemned.

This means God's forgiveness is not automatic. We do not obtain it by simply accepting Jesus' "finished work on the Cross." God appropriates the merits of Christ's propitiation to us only if we confess our sins with faith in His forgiveness. Remember, the New Covenant is not merely legal, but personal as well. It is based on faith, not law. There is a personal, dynamic relationship

---

[83] See, for example, Ex 30:12-16; 32:30; Num 25:11; 31:50; 2 Sam 21:1-14; Ps 65:3; 78:38; 79:9; 106:30; Is 27:9; 47:11; Dan 9:24; Jer 18:23; Ezek 16:63; 18:23; Zech 7:2; 8:22; Mal 1:9.

[84] 1 Jn 1:7-9.

between how we approach God after we sin (confession) and what Jesus does for us in return (propitiation). The New Covenant sacrifice applies only to *confessed* sins, and not present and future sins that may not be confessed and accompanied by repentance. If God did not require us to repent and confess our sins, Christ's Atonement would be merely a legal transaction and everyone would be saved.

This is why Peter makes a distinction between past sins and future sins: "For whoever lacks these things is blind and short-sighted and has forgotten that he was cleansed from his *old* sins" (2 Pet 1:9). Peter is referring to *past* sins that have been confessed and forgiven through the ongoing sacrifice of Christ. Future sins will need to be confessed so that Christ's atoning work can wash them away. Notice also that Peter, like John, uses the word "cleansed" to describe what happens to past, confessed sins.

Paul likewise says, "Where there is forgiveness of these, there is no longer any offering for sin" (Heb 10:18). Paul is also teaching that our past confessed sins no longer require atonement, *but our present and future unconfessed sins do*. If we confess our sins, the Father accepts Jesus' ongoing propitiatory offering to atone for those sins, and He expiates them in His mercy. These sins become "old sins" for which atonement is no longer required. There is a perfect harmony between the teachings of Peter, Paul, and John on how Christ's atoning work is applied to the sinner.

We also note that Paul refers to Jesus' "offering for sin" in the context of His heavenly appearance as "our great priest over the house of God."[85] Once again, Christ's heavenly priesthood and His sacrifice for sins are inseparable. Paul could make this connection only if Jesus *and His offering for sin* were present in the heavenly sanctuary.

---

[85] Heb 10:21; see also Heb 10:12.

What happens if we sin after we have been forgiven? We must confess our sins again. This is why Paul says:

> For if we sin deliberately after receiving the knowledge of the truth, there no longer remains a sacrifice for sins, but a fearful prospect of judgment, and a fury of fire which will consume the adversaries.[86]

While Paul repeatedly teaches that Christ's atoning sacrifice is being offered in heaven, he says that it no longer applies to those who commit deliberate sin. This again means that the application of Christ's sacrifice to sinners is not automatic. To avail ourselves of Christ's infinite merits, we have to approach our loving Father with a contrite heart and confess our new sins. Then the Father will expiate our sins and infuse grace into our souls.

This indicates why Paul writes to the Romans: "Since, therefore, we are now justified by his *blood*, much more shall we be saved by him from the *wrath* of God" (Rom 5:9). Paul's connection of averting God's wrath through the blood of Jesus describes the process of propitiation. Further, Paul speaks of Christ's blood in the present tense and our salvation in the future tense. This underscores the ongoing dynamic between Christ's shed blood, the Father's appeasement, and our salvation which we continue to "work out with fear and trembling" (Phil 2:12).

Thus, Scripture presents a threefold process in the application of Christ's atoning work: *confession, propitiation, and expiation*. We confess, Jesus propitiates, and the Father expiates. This is how we become perfected in the New Covenant. There is a dynamic relationship between our ongoing actions (sin and confession) and Jesus' ongoing mediation in heaven (propitiating the Father). This ongoing process is entirely at odds with the Protestant view that all sins — past, present, and future — have been forgiven by Christ's once-for-all sacrifice.

---

[86] Heb 10:26-27.

Confessing Sins

When John tells us that we must "confess our sins," he is referring to the sacrament of Confession, one of the seven sacraments of the New Covenant. Jesus conferred upon His apostles and their successors the authority to forgive sins so that those who approached God in faith could benefit from His heavenly intercession. John, who teaches us to confess our sins to be cleansed by Jesus' blood, records this event in his Gospel. After His Resurrection, Jesus appeared to His apostles and said:

> "As the Father has sent me, even so I send you." And when he had said this, he breathed on them, and said to them, "Receive the Holy Spirit. If you forgive the sins of any, they are forgiven; if you retain the sins of any, they are retained."
>
> — JN 20:21-23

While there could not be a more unmistakable way in which Jesus could have conferred the authority to forgiven sins upon the apostles, Protestants have trouble with the idea that men can forgive sins. They question the Apostle Matthew's statement that God had given the authority to forgive sin *"to men"* (Mt 9:8). Like the Pharisees, they cry, "Who can forgive sins but God alone?" (Mk 2:7). We can respond to the Protestant concern using both Scripture and logic.

The purpose of Christ's ministry on earth was to forgive sins. We see this from the very beginning, when the angel Gabriel told the Blessed Virgin Mary, "You shall call his name Jesus, for he will save his people from their sins" (Mt 1:21). Jesus said of His mission: "I have not come to call the righteous, but sinners to repentance."[87] John the Baptist saw Jesus and declared: "Behold, the Lamb of God, who takes away the sins of the world!"[88] Throughout the

---

[87] Lk 5:23; see also Mt 9:13; Mk 2:17.
[88] Jn 1:29; see also Jn 1:36.

Gospels, we see our loving Savior embracing all people and saying those beautiful words, "Your sins are forgiven."[89]

Is it not reasonable to conclude that Jesus would confer upon His Church the authority to continue the mission that He came to earth to achieve? Or was Jesus interested only in reconciling the sinners of His day, and not those of future generations? Jesus Himself answers our question by telling the apostles, "As the Father sent me, even so I send you" (Jn 20:21). If Jesus' divine mission was to restore all peoples to the Father, then Jesus had to provide the means by which those not living during His earthly life could be forgiven of sin. He did this by conferring the authority to forgive sins upon His apostles and their successors; the same authority that the Father gave Jesus while on Jesus was on earth.[90]

In the face of the plain meaning of Scripture, anti-Catholics may acknowledge that the apostles had this authority, but deny that it was transmitted to their successors. Such an argument denies the many Scriptures demonstrating that Christ invested His authority in the *office* of the apostles, and not merely in their private capacity as individuals. As Scripture teaches, these offices are held by the pope,[91] bishops,[92] and priests.[93] This is why Paul calls his position a divine "office" (Col 1:25).

Right before Jesus ascended into heaven, He told His apostles, "I am with you always, to the close of the age" (Mt 28:20). Since "the close of the age" refers to the end of time, and the apostles would not live on earth until the end, Jesus promised to be with the apostles *and their successors* "to the close of the age." If

---

[89] See Mt 9:2; Mk 2:5; Luke 5:20; 7:48.

[90] Mt 9:6; Mk 2:10; Lk 5:24.

[91] See Mt 16:18-19.

[92] See Acts 20:17, 28; Phil 1:1; 1 Tim 3:1; Titus 1:7.

[93] See Acts 20:17, 28; 1 Tim 5:17; Titus 1:5; Jas 5:14. The Church is also composed of deacons who assist the priests and serve the Christian community (see Phil 1:1; 1 Tim 3:8).

not, Jesus' promise that the "gates of hell" would not prevail against the Church would have been bogus and the Church would have perished with the apostles. Since the need to reconcile sinners to God exists today as much as it did during the apostolic age, the Church continues Christ's mission through the apostles' successors. These men have succeeded to the office of the apostles through a formal ordination ceremony called "the laying on of hands."[94]

Protestants are quick to point out that Catholic priests are only human beings and sinners, just like everyone else. As such, they have weaknesses and shortcomings. But Protestants must understand the distinction between the *office* of the priest and the *person* of the priest, as Scripture teaches. In a debate with a Protestant about the sacrament of Confession, I asked my opponent, "Can you pardon a criminal from a state prison like the governor can?" He admitted that he could not. I then pointed out to him that both he and the governor were merely human beings, yet one of them had the authority to pardon criminals. "Why is that?" I asked.

He acknowledged that the governor had a special office which gave him the pardoning authority. I then explained that this is the very same distinction the Church makes between the person of the priest and the office he holds.

The priest, in his *personal* capacity, has no more power than any other baptized Christian. But in his *official* capacity, as an ambassador of God, the priest exercises a power that transcends his human limitations. It is the very power of God himself. About his office as priest and the sacrament of Reconciliation, Paul says, "All this is from God, who through Christ reconciled us to himself and gave us the *ministry of reconciliation*; So we are *ambassadors* for Christ, God making his appeal through us."[95]

---

[94] See Acts 1:15-26; 6:5-6; 12:2-3; 1 Tim 4:4; 5:22; 2 Tim 1:6.
[95] 2 Cor 5:18, 20.

It is often difficult to confess one's inner secrets to another person. It is much easier to go "privately to God." But the sacrament of Penance is a necessary part of the personal dimensions of the New Covenant. God requires us to have faith not only in Him, but also in those that He has appointed over us. God has commanded us to "obey our leaders" who "keep watch over our souls" (Heb 13:17). God requires this faith and obedience in order to receive the benefits of the New Covenant, for it was the lack of faith and obedience that condemned us in the Old Covenant.

Further, God wants us to have an objective means by which we both come to grips with our sinfulness and obtain the knowledge that our sins are forgiven. This happens when we confess our sins and then hear the words of the priest: "I absolve you from your sins in the name of the Father, and of the Son, and of the Holy Spirit." This provides us a sense of comfort and assurance that no "secret" confession to God could possibly give us.

In Confession, we demonstrate our love for God. We approach Him in faith as our loving Father, not a merciless judge. When we do this, the Father cleanses us from our sins in the blood of His Son, which Jesus continually presents to Him before the throne in heaven. This is the blood that Jesus poured out for us on the Cross and that He continues to pour out before the Father through the Eucharistic sacrifice. In the next section, we look at how Jesus makes His sacrifice present on earth in the Holy Mass.

CHAPTER III
———

The Real Presence of Christ in the Eucharist

"THIS IS MY BODY; THIS IS MY BLOOD"

The night before He died, Jesus instituted the sacrament of the Eucharist as the sign and seal of the New Covenant. Jesus took bread, blessed and broke it, and said, "This is my body," and a cup of wine and said, "This is my blood." He then conferred the office of priesthood upon His apostles by commanding them: "Do this in memory of me."[1]

Jesus commanded His apostles to "do this" so that the merits of His propitiatory death could be appropriated to sinners throughout time and space. Those who come to the Eucharistic sacrifice with faith receive the grace of forgiveness and renew their covenant relationship with God. God forgives their sins and infuses their souls with sanctifying grace. In the state of grace, they are made pleasing to God and can have a gracious relationship with Him.

When a validly ordained priest obeys Jesus' command by celebrating the Eucharistic sacrifice in the Holy Mass, he acts *in persona Christi* (in the person of Christ). That is, he steps into the shoes of Jesus Christ and offers the same sacrifice that Jesus is offering the Father in heaven — the sacrifice of His Body and Blood. Because Jesus' heavenly priesthood is modeled after that of Melchizedek, Jesus, through His priest, offers His Body and

---

[1] Mt 26:26-28; Mk 14:22-24; Lk 22:19-20; 1 Cor 11:23-25.

Blood to the Father under the appearance of bread and wine. The faithful then consume Christ's Body and Blood in Holy Communion. The life of the early Church was centered on the celebration of the Eucharist, which it called "the breaking of the bread" (Acts 2:42). We begin by studying how Jesus instituted the Eucharist at the Last Supper.

The Words of Consecration

After Jesus took bread[2] and gave thanks, He said, "This is my body." All three Synoptic Gospels, as well as Paul's letter to the Corinthians, record these same words.[3] If Jesus wanted His apostles to believe that the bread actually became His Body, then His choice of words could not have been clearer. If He did not want to give His apostles this impression, then Jesus, the omnipotent Son of God, made a grammatical blunder of monumental proportions.

The gravity of such an error would be highlighted by the fact that Jesus was speaking on the eve of His Passion and death. He was communicating His last will and testament to His apostles and spoke like a dying father speaks to his grieving children on his deathbed. Such a solemn event would require Jesus to eliminate any ambiguity as He delivered His message, especially to eleven uneducated common men who hung on His every word and were now commissioned to carry on His mission. As Paul teaches, God cannot deceive us.[4]

---

[2] It is probable that Jesus received His own Body and Blood, for when Scripture says he "took" bread and wine (Mt 26:26; Mk 14:22; Lk 22:17,19; 1 Cor 11:23), it is likely that he took them in the same way as He gave the apostles to take. Jesus also said that He "earnestly desired to *eat* the passover" with His apostles before He consecrated the bread and wine (Lk 2:15). Christ was to fulfill what He required the faithful to observe, just as He did with prayer, fasting, and baptism.

[3] Mt 26:26; Mk 14:22; Lk 22:19; 1 Cor 11:24.

[4] Titus 1:2; Heb 6:18.

As we will see in the chapter on the Church Fathers, all the early Christians believed that Jesus spoke literally at the Last Supper, so that when the priest celebrates the Eucharist in His memory, the bread and wine become Jesus' Body and Blood. While they could not explain exactly how the miracle occurred (neither can we today), they believed the miracle did occur, based on Christ's simple words. Their belief in the Real Presence of Christ in the Eucharist was so strong that thousands of early Christians, including many children, chose torture and death rather than deny the doctrine.

Surely, Jesus Christ would have foreseen the shameful error into which He would have led the early Church had His words been metaphorical. In fact, Jesus would have been to blame for allowing such a gross error to infect the Church at its very beginnings. The reality is that no one even debated the meaning of Christ's words for the first ten centuries of the Church, and the doctrine of the Eucharist was not seriously questioned until the Protestant revolt in the sixteenth century.

Because the historical witness to the Eucharist is so compelling, Protestants are forced to argue that the Church got it all wrong for over 1,500 years — and that when Jesus said, "This is my body," He didn't really mean that the bread became His Body. To that end, Protestants offer the technical argument that the demonstrative adjective "this" in the phrase "this is my body" refers to the "bread," which is the object of the adjective. Because the bread cannot be both "bread" and Jesus' "body" at the same time, they argue that it must still be bread. Further, they contend, since the bread continues to look like bread, it only represents Jesus' body, but is not His literal Body.

Of course, if Jesus wanted to teach His apostles that the Eucharistic bread was a mere symbol of His Body, He could have said, "This means my body," or "This represents my body," or "This symbolizes my body." But He didn't. Jesus didn't even say,

"This becomes my body." He wanted to eliminate any debate about when the miracle actually occurred, emphasizing instead that the change was instantaneous.[5] Even if none of these things was true, however, the Protestant argument is defeated by an analysis of the Greek grammar.

An Analysis of the Greek

The Greek transliteration of "This is my body which is given for you" in Lk 22:19 is *Touto esti to soma mou to uper hymon didomenon*. Like many languages, Greek adjectives have genders (masculine, feminine, or neuter) which agree with their object nouns. The word "this" (*touto*) is a neuter adjective. The word "bread" (*artos*) is a masculine noun. This means that the neuter adjective "this" is not referring to the masculine noun "bread," because their genders do not correspond. Instead, "this" refers to "body" (*soma*), which is a neuter noun. In light of the grammatical structure, Jesus does not say "This bread is my body," as the Protestant argument contends. Instead, Jesus says "This [*new substance*] is my body," or more literally, "This [*new substance*] is the body of me."

Paul emphasizes the connection between "this" and Jesus' "body" even more conspicuously. In 1 Cor 11:24, Paul records Jesus' words as *Touto mou esti to soma*. As we can see, *mou* (of me) comes immediately after *touto* (this). Literally, this phrase is translated as "This of me is the body." That is, Paul connects "this" to the Person of Jesus more closely by adding "of me" right after "this" and right before "body." Again, the Greek does not allow

---

[5] The change is instantaneous because it is brought about by the power of God's Word. Because God's Word is infinite, it is not bound by temporal and spatial limitations. Jesus' choice of words ("this is. . .") emphasizes that transubstantiation is an act of divine power. We see this when Jesus cured the deaf and dumb man by saying, "*Ephpheta*, which is, Be thou opened. And *immediately* his ears were opened, and the string of his tongue was loosed" (Mk 7:34-35 [DR]).

"this" to refer to the bread, but to the new substance, which is Jesus' body.

Mt 26:28 uses the same grammatical construction in reference to Christ's blood. The Greek transliteration of "This is my blood" is *Touto gar estin to haima mou*. Again, "this" (*touto*) is a neuter adjective which corresponds to the neuter noun "blood" (*haima*), not the masculine noun "wine" (*oinos*). Matthew, Luke and Paul, under the inspiration of the Holy Spirit, were meticulous in ensuring that the demonstrative adjective "this" (*touto*) referred to Christ's Body and Blood, and not to the bread and wine.

It should also be noted that in the Four Gospels, the phrase "this is" (*touto esti*) is used another six times outside the Last Supper accounts.[6] In each instance, the object noun is always literal. For example, Jesus says:

- "*This is* the great and first commandment" (Mt 22:38).
- "*This is* the work of God" (Jn 6:29).
- "*This is* my commandment" (Jn 15:12).

The Apostle John also writes:

- *This is* the testimony of John (Jn 1:19).
- And *this is* the judgment (Jn 3:19).

In each of these cases, the demonstrative adjective and finite verb "this is" is always followed by a literal object noun. The Gospel writers never follow the phrase *touto esti* with a metaphor. Thus, the Protestant argument that Jesus was speaking metaphorically when He said "this is" has no precedent in the Gospels.

The Catholic understanding of Jesus' words is supported by a further analysis of the Greek language. When Jesus said, "This is my body which is given for you," the appositional phrase "is

---

[6] Mt 22:38; 27:46; Jn 1:19; 3:19; 6:29; 15:12. The Latin Vulgate translates "this is" as *hoc est*. Thus, in the official Latin text of the Mass, the priest says, "*Hoc est enim corpus meum*" (This is my body).

given for you" (*didomenon*) is a present participle in Greek. The tense of participles is determined by the tense of the main verb. If the main verb is in the present tense (here, the present indicative "is"), then the participle is also present tense ("is given for you").

As applied here, Jesus' use of the double present tense means that, as He spoke the words, He was literally giving His Body to His apostles. Although Protestants may argue that Christ was referring to His future death, such grammatical usage in New Testament Greek does not refer to a future event. Paul also records Jesus as saying "This is my body which is broken for you" (1 Cor 11:24). The Greek word for "broken" (*klomenon*) is another present participle which describes the tense of an action that is simultaneous with the main verb "is." This usage limits Christ's words to the strictly present, highlighting that Jesus was currently offering His broken body as an unbloody sacrifice in the Upper Room.

That Jesus consecrated the bread first, and then the wine, also indicates that He was offering His Body in sacrifice. When blood is separated from the body, death occurs. Jesus presumably isolated the consecrations of the bread and wine to signify the separation of His Body and Blood, so that when the priest acts *in persona Christi*, Christ's immolated state is made present. As we have learned, Jesus desires His sacrifice to be made present so that those who approach the sacrifice in faith may receive its grace-filled benefits.

When Jesus took the cup of wine and gave thanks, He said, "Drink of it, all of you; for this is my blood of the covenant, which is poured out for many for the forgiveness of sins."[7] As with Jesus' "body," Matthew and Mark use the finite verb "is"

---

[7] Matt 26:27-28; Mark 14:24. The Greek transliteration is *Touto gar estin to haima mou to tes kaines diathekes to peri pollon ekchynnomenon eis aphesin hamartion.*

(*estin*) and the present participle "is poured out" (*ekchynnomenon*) to describe what is happening to Jesus' blood. As we saw with the phrase "is given for you," when such a double present tense is used in New Testament Greek, the time described is always the present tense, not the future. This means that Jesus was pouring out His Blood in sacrifice at the Last Supper.

Matthew's Gospel fortifies this conclusion by connecting the "pouring out" of Jesus' blood with the "forgiveness of sin." Recall that Paul says, "Without the shedding of blood there is no forgiveness of sins" (Heb 9:22). This demonstrates that the Eucharist is a propitiatory sacrifice to God to forgive sin through the shedding of blood. That is the purpose and effect of the Eucharistic sacrifice.

Notice also that in Matthew and Mark's Gospels, Jesus says, "This is my blood of the covenant." The phrase "blood of the covenant" is identical to the phrase Moses used when he sprinkled the Israelites with the blood of the animal sacrifices to ratify the Old Covenant: "Behold, *the blood of the covenant.*"[8] It seems plausible that Jesus deliberately used this phrase to emphasize that He was pouring His blood out in sacrifice at the moment He uttered the words, just as Moses poured the blood upon the people while using the same words. The Jewish apostles would have understood immediately that Jesus was instituting, at that very moment, a New Covenant sacrifice that would replace the Old Covenant sacrifices.

Some Protestants argue that Jesus' words were metaphorical by pointing to Luke and Paul's respective recording of Jesus' words: "This cup which is poured out for you is the new covenant in my blood" (Lk 22:20); "This cup is the new covenant in my blood" (1 Cor 11:25). In Luke and Paul's account, Jesus says the "cup" is the "new covenant." Because the "cup" is not literally the "new

---

[8] Ex 24:8; in Greek, *Idou to haima tes diathekes.*

covenant," many Protestants contend that Jesus' words at the Last
Supper were figurative only, representing the spiritual truth that
Jesus was implementing a New Covenant, but not the literal truth
that He was shedding His blood in making the covenant.

There are a number of problems with this point of view.
First, as we have learned from Matthew and Mark's Gospels,
Jesus is referring to His blood being poured out *in the present
tense*. That Luke and Paul record the "cup" as the "covenant"
does not change this fact. Second, whether we call the "cup" or
the "blood" the covenant is not relevant to whether the blood
is literally or figuratively being poured out. That is because neither the "cup" nor the "blood" is the actual covenant. The
covenant is the *promise* that God swore through the eternal
priesthood of Jesus Christ to grant those salvation that came to
Him in faith.

In calling the "cup" the covenant in Jesus' blood, Luke and
Paul are using a common biblical literary device called a *synecdoche*. A synecdoche is a figure of speech which represents the
thing it symbolizes. According to Matthew and Mark's Gospels,
through the use of the double present tense, Jesus is currently
pouring out His blood of the covenant. The "cup" simply represents the *actual* blood of the covenant that Jesus is offering. It in
no way converts the otherwise literal words of Jesus into figurative words.

In fact, Luke's connection of the "cup" with "is poured out"
highlights the sacrificial language in a more striking way. In Luke's
account, Jesus' shedding of blood (*ekchynnomenon*) actually takes
place in the cup (*poterion*). That is, Jesus connects the "shedding"
with the cup, and not His Blood. This wording emphasizes that
Jesus' blood is being *separated* from His Body, since the separation
occurs *in the cup*. Luke isolates the shedding of blood to the cup
to underscore that Jesus' death is truly made present under the
separate consecrations of the bread and wine.

"Offer This as My Memorial Sacrifice"

If the apostles had any doubts about the sacrificial nature of Jesus' words, Jesus eliminated those doubts when He told them, "Do this in remembrance of me."[9] The Greek word for "remembrance" is *anamnesis,* which refers to a "memorial sacrifice."[10] Thus, Jesus literally commanded His apostles to "Offer this as my memorial sacrifice."

A memorial sacrifice is not a mere remembrance of a past event. It is a *sacrifice* that brings about remembrance. In other words, the memorial dimension exists only because the sacrifice brings it about. As applied here, the memorial sacrifice of the Eucharist prompts God to "remember" Christ's one sacrifice *because it is re-presented to Him.* As a result, God responds to the sacrifice for the very reason Christ offered it in the first place: to appease the Father's wrath so that He would dispense His grace and forgiveness.

To anticipate the facile objection, we acknowledge that reminding God about Christ's sacrifice does not mean that God forgets things. Rather, it implores God's immediate attention to the matter at hand and asks for His gracious response. Such is the case when we offer God our prayers. God already knows our needs but desires that we demonstrate our faith by beseeching Him as our loving Father, not our merciless Lawgiver. As we have already stated, the New Covenant is not legal, but personal. God's dealings with us are not mechanical, but paternal.

Many Protestants maintain that the Last Supper could not have been a re-presentation of Christ's death because His death

---

[9] Lk 22:19; 1 Cor 11:25. The Greek transliteration is *Touto poiete eis tan emain anamnesin.*

[10] In Hebrew, this Greek term comes from *zikaron (zakar)*, which in the context of the Passover had a real sense of making the event "truly present," not simply a calling to mind or a memorial in the common sense of the term.

had not yet occurred. First, Catholics do not claim that the Last Supper was a re-presentation of Christ's death; it was a *prototype* of the death that was to occur the next day. Thus, the Protestant raises a straw man argument. Christ's actions at the Last Supper do not differ from His implementation of the sacraments of Baptism (Jn 3:5) or Confession (Jn 20:23) before their formal inauguration on Pentecost Sunday.

Second, when Christ commanded His apostles to "do this" in His memory, He was obviously pointing to future celebrations of the Eucharist. These *future* celebrations would bring about the re-presentation of His Calvary sacrifice, which is what the Catholic Church maintains. In this sense, the Protestant argument does not address what the Church actually teaches.

Third, although Christ's death had not yet occurred, God can apply the merits of His sacrifice in advance of its actual occurrence. As we have seen, Christ's sacrifice was secured "from the foundation of the world."[11] Since Christ's sacrifice was certain to occur (here, the very next day), God could make present the offering of His Body and Blood in the Upper Room before they were offered on the Cross.

An Analysis of the Greek

The Greek grammar demonstrates that the Eucharist is the sacrifice of Christ's Body and Blood. When Jesus said, "Do this in remembrance of me," the word "this" (*touto*) has no referent in that phrase (Lk 22:19).[12] This requires us to look back to the action of the preceding sentence to understand what "this" refers to. The preceding sentence is: "This is my body which is given for you" (v. 19). This means that "do this" refers to the "giving" of Jesus' body, which makes the giving a sacrifice.

---

[11] See Apoc 13:8; Heb 4:3.

[12] See also 1 Cor 11:25. The Greek literally says "this do" (*touto poiete*), which makes Jesus' statement emphatic.

The Catholic understanding of the Eucharist as a sacrifice becomes even more compelling when we look at Luke and Paul's use of the Greek word *anamnesis* for "remembrance." While there are more than a handful of Greek words that can describe a "remembrance" of something, *anamnesis* is the only word that refers *exclusively to a sacrifice*.

Outside of Luke and Paul's Last Supper accounts, *anamnesis* appears only one other time in the New Testament, where Paul uses it in Heb 10:3: "But in these sacrifices there is a *reminder (anamnesis)* of sin year after year." In this verse, Paul is referring to the sin offerings under the Old Covenant Levitical laws.[13] In these offerings, it was the *sacrifice itself* that brought about the "remembrance" of sin to the Israelites and made atonement for those sins.[14]

There are two primary places where the Greek *anamnesis* is used in the Septuagint translation of the Old Testament: Num 10:10 and Lev 24:7. In these cases, *anamnesis* refers to an actual sacrifice to bring about a remembrance. Moreover, the sacrifices involved the offerings of *both bread and blood*. It is therefore no surprise why Luke and Paul used *anamnesis* to describe the Eucharistic sacrifice — a *blood* sacrifice under the appearance of wine and *bread*.

---

[13] See, for example, Lev 4:3, 8, 14, 20-21, 24-25, 29, 32-34; 5:6-9, 11-12; 6:17, 25, 30; 7:7, 37; 8:2, 14; 9:2-3, 7-8, 10, 15, 22; 10:16-17, 19; 12:6, 8; 14:13, 19, 22, 31; 15:15, 30; 16:3, 5, 6, 9, 11, 25, 27; 23:19.

[14] Because the Levitical sacrifices were designed to remind the Israelites of their sins, their consciences could not be made completely clean. This is why, in the preceding verse (Heb 10:2), Paul says, "If the worshipers had once been cleansed, they would no longer have any consciousness of sin." About the Old Covenant system, Paul also says, "According to this arrangement, gifts and sacrifices are offered which cannot perfect the conscience of the worshiper" (Heb 9:9). Paul's point is that the Old Covenant law was designed to *highlight* the people's sin, and the New Covenant of grace is designed to *remove* sin. Thus, Paul teaches that "through the law comes knowledge of sin" (Rom 3:20), but now, through "the blood of Christ," we are able to "purify our conscience" to serve the living God (Heb 9:14).

The *anamnesis* bread-sacrifice occurs in Lev 24:7-9:

> And you shall put pure *frankincense* with each row, that it
> may go with the *bread* as a *memorial* (*anamnesis*) portion to
> be *offered* by fire to the LORD. Every *sabbath* day Aaron shall
> set it in order before the LORD *continually* on behalf of the
> people of Israel as a *covenant for ever*. And it shall be for
> *Aaron and his sons*, and they shall *eat* it in a *holy place*, since
> it is for him a most *holy portion* out of the *offerings* by fire
> to the LORD, a *perpetual due*.

In this short passage, we see familiar Eucharistic terminology:
incense, bread, memorial, continual sacrifice, priests, covenant, and
eat. Notice that the bread sacrifice is a perpetual sacrifice that is
to be offered every Sabbath day as an eternal covenant. The sacrifice is offered by priests (Aaron and his sons) who eat the sacrifice in a holy place. These elements clearly correspond to the
Eucharist: a perpetual sacrifice, offered under the appearance of
bread, every Sabbath (Sunday) as the New and Eternal Covenant.
The sacrifice is offered by priests who eat the sacrifice in a holy
place (the church). The sacrifice brings about the "remembrance"
of sin and God's forgiveness of that sin.

The *anamnesis* blood-sacrifice occurs in Num 10:10:

> On the day of your gladness also, and at your appointed
> feasts, and at the beginnings of your months, you shall blow
> the trumpets over your *burnt offerings* and over the sacrifices
> of your peace offerings; they shall serve you for *remembrance*
> (*anamnesis*) before your God: I am the LORD your God.

In this passage, "burnt offerings" bring about the "remembrance" before God of the people's sin and God's forgiveness of
that sin. These burnt offerings involved both the shedding of
blood and its presentation on the altar of sacrifice to make atonement for sin. For example, in the book of Leviticus we read:

He shall lay his hand upon the head of the *burnt offering*, and it shall be accepted for him to make *atonement* for him. Then he shall *kill* the bull before the LORD; and Aaron's sons the *priests* shall present the *blood*, and throw the *blood* round about against the *altar* that is at the door of the *tent* of meeting. And the priest shall burn the whole on the *altar*, as a *burnt offering*, an offering by fire, a *pleasing odor* to the LORD.[15]

Once again, we see familiar Eucharistic terminology and symbolism: *priests, sacrifice, death, atonement, blood, altar,* and *tent* or *sanctuary*. We also see that the sacrifice is a "pleasing odor" to the Lord, which is the same description Paul uses to describe the sacrifice of Christ: "Christ loved us and gave himself up for us, a fragrant offering and sacrifice to God" (Eph 5:2).

Along with "burnt offerings," Num 10:10 also mentions "peace offerings" which bring about the "remembrance" (*anamnesis*). Peace offerings included "thanksgiving" offerings, from which we get the word "Eucharist."[16] The thanksgiving offering would include a sacrifice involving *both bread and blood*. In Lev 7:13, we see the thank offering of bread:

With the sacrifice of his peace offerings for *thanksgiving* he shall bring his offering with cakes of leavened *bread*.

In the next two verses, we see the thanksgiving *blood* offering, where an animal is slain and its flesh is eaten:

And of such he shall offer one cake from each offering, as an offering to the Lord; it shall belong to the priest who throws the *blood* of the peace offerings. And the *flesh* of the

---

[15] Lev 1:4-5, 9. Remember, these were the same sacrifices offered by Noah, Job, and Abraham, men who were justified by grace, not law.

[16] In Greek, *eucharistein*; in Hebrew, *toda*.

sacrifice of his peace offerings for *thanksgiving* shall be eaten
on the day of his offering.

— Lev 7:14-15

Because the Old Covenant thanksgiving sacrifices involved
both bread and blood, it was natural for the early Church to call
the New Covenant sacrifice the "Eucharist." In the Eucharist, the
bread and wine are changed into the Body and Blood of Christ
through sacrifice, and the flesh of Christ is eaten in thanksgiving
to God. Jesus himself connected the Old Covenant thank offerings to the Eucharist when He "gave thanks" as He offered His
Body and Blood.[17] It is no surprise that Paul, after expounding on
Jesus' heavenly blood sacrifice in his letter to the Hebrews, fin-
ishes his letter by saying, "Through him then let us continually
offer up a *sacrifice of praise*" (Heb 13:15).[18] The "sacrifice of
praise" is the New Covenant thanksgiving offering of the Holy
Eucharist.

Through the use of the word *anamnesis* in the Last Supper
accounts, Luke and Paul deliberately connect the Eucharist to the
bread and blood sacrifices of the Old Covenant. In so doing,
Luke and Paul were communicating that the Eucharist is *also* a
sacrifice involving bread and blood. But, unlike the Old
Covenant sacrifices, which prompted remembrance of sin and
appeased God only temporarily, the New Covenant sacrifice propitiates God completely, for it perpetually makes present to Him
the perfect sacrifice of His divine Son.

The Greek word *anamnesis* comes from the Hebrew word
zakar. Another Greek word for sacrifice, *mnemosunon*, is also
taken from the Hebrew *zakar*. Unlike *anamnesis*, *mnemosunon*
can refer either to a bloody sacrifice, an unbloody sacrifice, or a
nonsacrificial memorial. For example:

---

[17] Mt 26:27; Mk 14:23; Lk 22:17, 19; 1 Cor 11:23.
[18] See also Ps 116:17.

- Ex 12:14 refers to the memorial of a blood sacrifice of a lamb: "This day shall be for you a *memorial* day, and you shall keep it as a feast to the LORD."
- Lev 2:2 refers to the memorial of a nonbloody cereal offering: "the priest shall burn this as its *memorial* portion upon the altar."
- Neh 5:19 refers to a nonsacrificial memorial: "*Remember* for my good, O my God, all that I have done for this people."
- Mt 26:13 also refers to a nonsacrificial memorial: "What she has done will be told in *memory* of her."

Why is this important? Because in describing the memorial of the Eucharist, Luke and Paul chose the one word that refers *exclusively* to *blood sacrifice*: *anamnesis*. Although the Greek language gave them other options, Luke and Paul made it clear that the Eucharist was a propitiatory sacrifice for sins, and not a mere pious remembrance of a past event or a fellowship meal.[19]

To counter the Church's teaching that the Cross and the Mass are the same sacrifice, some Protestants point out that one can attend Mass every day of his life and still not make it to heaven. This seems to mean to them that the Mass is an ineffectual sacrifice, and therefore cannot be the same sacrifice as that of the Cross. However, this argument fails to recognize that the Cross alone is equally ineffectual for everyone: not all people make it to heaven. The issue is not with the *efficacy* of the sacrifice, but with the *faith* that one must place in the sacrifice. If one does not have faith in the sacrifice of the Cross, he receives no benefit from it. It is the same with the sacrifice of the Mass. One needs personal faith in the New Covenant sacrifice to receive God's gift of grace and forgiveness.

---

[19] In fact, Paul says that the Eucharist is not a fellowship meal when he says, "When you meet together, it is not the Lord's supper that you eat" (1 Cor 11:20).

To deny the need for the Mass, some Protestants also refer to Jesus' statement to the Pharisees, "I desire mercy, and not sacrifice."[20] This argument not only ignores Jesus' command to offer the memorial sacrifice in His memory, but wrenches Jesus' statement entirely out of context. The Pharisees were accusing Jesus of sin for curing a man and allowing His disciples to pick grain on the Sabbath. In response, Jesus indicted the Pharisees for their scrupulous legalism and utter lack of faith in God. If they were to be saved, they would have to abandon their legal rituals (Levitical sacrifices) and come to God in faith (by changing their hearts and showing mercy toward others). Again, Jesus is emphasizing that faith is the portal to the New Covenant. Jesus' statement had nothing to do with the Eucharistic sacrifice.

In his letter to the Galatians, Paul uses different terminology to describe the "remembrance" of the Eucharistic sacrifice. After explaining the difference between the law of the Old Covenant and the grace of the New Covenant,[21] Paul says:

> O foolish Galatians! Who has bewitched you, before whose *eyes* Jesus Christ *was publicly portrayed as crucified?*
> — GAL 3:1

Paul then provides further analysis on the distinction between faith which leads to grace and law which leads to death (Gal 3:2-29).

The Galatians saw Jesus "publicly portrayed as crucified" during their celebrations of the Eucharistic sacrifice. The Greek word for "publicly portrayed" (*prographo*) describes a graphic

---

[20] Mt 9:13; 12:7. When God says He does not desire sacrifice, He is referring to sacrifices offered by faithless and disobedient people (see, for example, 1 Sam 15:22; Is 1:10-17; 40:6-8; Jer 7:21-26; Hos 8:11-13; and Amos 5:22-24). These Scripture verses do not contradict other verses, where God says He is pleased with sacrifice.

[21] See Gal 2:15-21.

depiction of something. In some cases, the word can refer to something that has been written down.[22] However, Paul couples *prographo* with the word *ophthalmos* in reference to the Galatians' *eyes* (as opposed to their ears or minds).[23]

In the New Testament, the word *ophthalmos* refers to the human eye or visually seeing something with the eye.[24] This means that the Galatians *actually saw with their own eyes* a graphic depiction of the Crucifixion (as opposed to merely listening to preaching about it or contemplating it in their minds). This is precisely what happens in the sacrifice of the Mass: Christ's crucifixion is visually re-presented under the appearance of bread and wine.

Paul brackets his statement in Gal 3:1 by a catechesis on law versus grace. In fact, Gal 3:1 appears right in the middle of Paul's grace/law dissertation (Gal 2:15 - 3:29). Evidently, even though the Galatians were celebrating the Eucharist, they were approaching the sacrament mechanically, and not faithfully. Like the Jews of the Old Covenant, their religion was becoming one based on works and not grace. This is why Paul calls the Galatians "foolish" and "bewitched" (Gal 3:1), and then asks them if they received the Spirit by "works of law" or by "faith" (Gal 3:2-5). Paul is warning the Galatians to approach the sacraments, especially the Eucharist, with personal faith because faith is the foundation of the New Covenant.

The Fruit of the Vine

Attempting to rebut the doctrine of the Eucharist, some Protestant apologists often refer us to the Last Supper narratives in Matthew and Mark's Gospels. In these accounts, after Jesus consecrated the wine into His "blood of the covenant," He said:

---

[22] See, for example, Rom 15:4; Eph 3:3.

[23] The Greek transliteration is *kata ophthalmos iesous Christos prographo stauroo*.

[24] See, for example, Mt 13:16; 17:8; 20:34; Mk 8:25; Lk 4:20; 6:20; 16:23; 24:31; Jn 6:5; 9:6, 10-11, 14-15, 17, 21, 26, 30, 32; 10:21; 11:37; 11:41; 17:1.

"I tell you I shall not drink again of this fruit of the vine until that day when I drink it new with you in my Father's kingdom."[25]

Because Jesus refers to His Blood as "the fruit of the vine," the Protestant contends that the contents in the cup remained wine. There are several problems with this argument.

First, while Matthew and Mark record Jesus' "fruit of the vine" statement as coming after His consecration of the bread and wine, the Protestant argument ignores Luke's Gospel, in which Jesus' statement occurs *before* the consecration. This means there is some ambiguity concerning the actual timing of Jesus' statement. Nevertheless, Luke's Gospel appears to provide the correct timing of the statement, because Luke specifically connects Jesus' statement with His eating of the common Passover meal.[26]

At the beginning of the Last Supper account, Luke records:

And when the hour came, he sat at table, and the apostles with him. And he said to them, "'I have earnestly desired to eat this passover with you before I suffer; for I tell you I shall not eat it until it is fulfilled in the kingdom of God."
— Lk 22:14-16

The "it" about which Jesus speaks refers to the unconsecrated Passover food of the preceding clause, not the bread of the Eucharist which Jesus had yet to consecrate. Luke's is the only Gospel that records Jesus' statement about not "eating" until the kingdom of God has come (Matthew and Mark's Gospels record only Jesus' statement about not "drinking").

In the next two verses, Jesus says the same thing with regard to the Passover wine:

---

[25] Mt 26:29; Mk 14:25.
[26] Because the Last Supper occurred on Preparation Day (Nisan 14) and not the actual Passover (Nisan 15), it is unclear whether Jesus and His apostles were actually celebrating the Passover Seder meal before the Last Supper.

> And he took a cup, and when he had given thanks he said,
> "Take this, and divide it among yourselves; for I tell you
> that from now on I shall not drink of the fruit of the vine
> until the kingdom of God comes."

> — Lk 22:17-18

Again, Jesus makes this statement *before* He consecrates either the bread or the wine into His Body and Blood.

Matthew's and Mark's Gospels *also* record that Jesus and His apostles were eating the Passover meal *before* Jesus instituted the Eucharist.[27] In light of the foregoing, it is most reasonable to conclude that Jesus' statements about "not eating or drinking" referred to the common food that He and His apostles were consuming during the Passover meal. Jesus was simply telling His apostles that His death was near, and He would not have any more time to dine with them until after His Resurrection.[28]

Second, even if Jesus referred to His Blood as the "fruit of the vine," this poses no problem for Catholic teaching. The Greek word for "fruit" is *genneema,* which literally means "that which is generated from the vine." Since Jesus refers to Himself as "the vine," then the "fruit of the vine" can also mean Jesus' blood.[29] Scripture also shows that *genneema* can also mean "birth" or "generation."[30] Since Jesus' "blood" gives "birth" to new life, Jesus can refer to His Blood as "fruit of the vine."

Further, Paul uses "bread" and "the body of the Lord" interchangeably in the same sentence when writing about the Eucharist (1 Cor 11:26-27). If Paul can refer to Christ's literal body as "bread," then Jesus can refer to His Blood as "fruit of the vine." Since Scripture provides other examples of things that have changed into something else but can still be called what they

---

[27] See Mt 26:26; 14:22.
[28] See Lk 24:42; Jn 21:13; Acts 10:41.
[29] See Jn 15:1, 5.
[30] See, for example, Mt 3:7; 12:34; 23:33.

originally were, Jesus' use of "fruit of the vine" does nothing for the Protestant position.[31]

A Living Sacrifice

Protestants often contend that there can be no sacrifice without suffering and death. They refer to Paul's statement in his letter to the Hebrews that "without the shedding of blood there is no forgiveness of sins" (Heb 9:22). Since Christ doesn't repeatedly die in heaven or in the Mass, Protestants argue that the Mass cannot be a sacrifice.

The Protestant argument erroneously assumes that sacrifices must always involve blood and death. This is not true. Not all the Levitical sacrifices (such as cereal offerings) involved killing animals and shedding blood. Aaron offered the Levites as a "wave offering" to God, an unbloody sacrifice.[32] Prayer and fasting (as we saw with Moses) is also a sacrifice in God's eyes to which God responds with mercy and forgiveness.

In the New Testament, Paul tells the Romans "to present your bodies as a *living* sacrifice, holy and acceptable to God, which is your spiritual worship" (Rom 12:1). Peter similarly exhorts us "to offer *spiritual* sacrifices acceptable to God through Jesus Christ" (1 Pet 2:5). Thus, the Scriptures teach that sacrifices do not always involve the shedding of blood. Sacrifices can be unbloody and life-giving.

The Eucharist is an unbloody and living sacrifice. It is an unbloody sacrifice because it re-enacts Christ's once-for-all blood sacrifice under sacramental signs, in the same manner as Melchizedek. It is a living sacrifice because it is offered by "the living one" who died and is alive forevermore (Apoc 1:18). It is also a life-giving sacrifice because it propitiates the Father, who grants grace to all who participate in the sacrifice with faith. Through

---

[31] See, for example, Gen 2:23; Ex 7:12; Jn 2:9; 2 Pet 2:22.
[32] See Num 8:11, 13, 15, 21.

Jesus, we continually offer up this "sacrifice of praise" and receive the gracious benefits of the New Covenant (see Heb 13:15).

PAUL'S TEACHING ON THE REAL PRESENCE

Paul provides us with some of the most profound insights in all of Scripture regarding the mystery of the Eucharist. As we have seen, in his letter to the Hebrews Paul addresses the major themes of Christ's heavenly priesthood, for example:

- how it is eternal
- how it is connected to the priesthood of Melchizedek
- how through it, Jesus mediates the New Covenant in order to save us
- how Jesus as High Priest has "something to offer" in heaven
- how in His offering, Jesus takes His Blood into the heavenly sanctuary
- how His Blood "speaks" to the Father on our behalf
- how Jesus appears once-for-all in heaven to offer "better sacrifices" than those of the Old Covenant
- how we must meet together to celebrate the sacrifice and eat at the altar
- how neglecting to meet together means we profane the blood of the covenant

Let us now turn to Paul's other teachings on the Eucharist.

Guilty of the Body and Blood of the Lord

When Paul wrote about the Eucharist in his letter to the Corinthians, he wanted them to know that he was simply handing on to them what he had received directly from Jesus Christ. In other words, Paul wanted the Corinthians to know that these were not his own ideas. Right before Paul writes about the institution of the Eucharist, Paul says, "For I received from the Lord what I also delivered to you" (1 Cor 11:23).

Paul then provides the narrative:

> The Lord Jesus on the night when he was betrayed took bread, and when he had given thanks, he broke it and said, "This is my body which is for you. Do this in remembrance of me." In the same way also the cup, after supper, saying, "This cup is the new covenant in my blood. Do this, as often as you drink it, in remembrance of me."
>
> (vv. 23-25)

Paul's account of the Last Supper closely follows the accounts recorded in the three synoptic Gospels. However, in the next three verses (26-30), Paul provides the Corinthians an interpretation of Jesus' words that the Gospels do not contain. First, Paul says, "For as often as you eat this bread and drink the cup, you proclaim the Lord's *death* until he comes" (v. 26).

The Greek word for "death" (*thanatos*) is the same word the Gospels use to describe Jesus' actual death on the cross.[33] Paul is not describing a lighthearted fellowship meal. He doesn't even mention the happy occasions of Jesus' Resurrection and Ascension. The Eucharist proclaims the *death* of Christ, which is the same thing as saying it proclaims *His sacrifice*. Thus, celebrating the Eucharist means offering the sacrifice of Christ "until he comes." If Jesus' "coming" is real, then the "sacrifice" is real as well. We proclaim one (Christ's death) in expectation of the other (Christ's coming).

In vv. 27-30, Paul completes his interpretation in the form of a startling warning about what will happen to the Corinthians if they partake of the Eucharist unworthily. Paul writes:

---

[33] Mt 20:18; 26:38; 26:66; Mk 10:33; 14:34, 64; Lk 24:20; Jn 11:13; 12:33; 18:32; 21:19.

Whoever, therefore, eats the bread or drinks the cup of the Lord in an unworthy manner will be guilty of profaning the body and blood of the Lord. Let a man examine himself, and so eat of the bread and drink of the cup. For any one who eats and drinks without discerning the body eats and drinks judgment upon himself. That is why many of you are weak and ill, and some have died.

— 1 COR 11:27-30

If the Corinthians had any doubt about the Real Presence of Christ in the Eucharist, Paul removed that doubt with this warning. Those who would presume to receive Christ's blood unworthily would be guilty of the most heinous crime of shedding that blood.[34] Let's unpack this critical passage.

The word "unworthy" (Greek, *anaxios*) means "unfit" or "incompetent." It is used only one other time in the New Testament, by Paul, to describe the inability or incompetence of the litigious Corinthians to judge civil matters among themselves as Christian brothers (1 Cor 6:2). If the Eucharist were mere bread and wine, then Paul would not accuse the Corinthians of being "unfit" or "incompetent" to eat the bread and drink the wine. One does not need special competence to eat and drink common food, for eating and drinking are natural actions.

The word "guilty" (Greek, *enochos*) refers to the guilt of a crime or penalty that is worthy of punishment. It is the same word the Pharisees used when they accused Jesus of the crime of

---

[34] A person becomes guilty of the Lord's Body and Blood when he receives the Eucharist in mortal sin, which is a grave sacrilege. A mortal sin requires three elements: (1) it deals with grave matter; (2) the person committing the sin knows it is grave and sufficiently reflects upon the act before committing the sin; (3) the person engages the full consent of his will and commits the sin. If a person has committed a mortal sin, that person must be absolved of the sin in the sacrament of Confession before receiving Holy Communion. The Apostle John wrote about the distinction between mortal and non-mortal sin in his first letter (1 Jn 5:16-17).

blasphemy: "He is *guilty* of death."[35] Some Protestants actually argue that the "guilt" Paul imputes to the Corinthians is for the sinful way in which they were treating each other. It is true that, right before their Eucharistic celebrations, the Corinthians would often eat a common meal, get drunk, and be abusive toward each other. However, when we examine the Greek, Paul connects the Corinthians' guilt or liability *directly* to Christ's Body and Blood: "liable shall be of the body and of the blood of the Lord" (*enochos eimi ho soma kai ho haima ho kurios*). Paul doesn't even remotely connect the Corinthians' guilt to their behavior toward each other.

Moreover, Paul says that the crime for such "guilt" is "judgment." The word "judgment" (Greek, *krima*) refers to nothing less than *eternal condemnation*. Paul uses the same word in his letter to the Romans when he describes the eternal consequences of Adam's sin: "For the judgment following one trespass brought condemnation" (Rom 5:16). Paul also warns bishops not to "fall into the condemnation of the devil" (1 Tim 3:6).[36] For those who do evil and call it good, Paul says "their condemnation is just" (Rom 3:8). Thus, when Paul says a person who receives the Eucharist unworthily eats and drinks "judgment" (*krima*) upon himself, he seems to indicate that such a person *has condemned himself to hell*.

If the Eucharist were just a symbol, Paul's punishment for receiving it unworthily is outrageous. We cannot be guilty of eternal damnation for abusing a symbol. We cannot be guilty of committing a crime against Christ's Body and Blood unless His Body and Blood are present. One cannot be guilty of committing a sin

---

[35] See Mt 26:66; Mk 14:64. Jesus connects such "guilt" with eternal "judgment" (Mt 5:21-22; Mk 3:29).

[36] See also Mt 7:2; 23:14; Mk 12:40; Lk 20:47; 23:40; Jn 9:39; Rom 2:2-3; 3:8; 1 Tim 3:6; 5:12; Heb 6:2; Jas 3:1; 1 Pet 4:17; 2 Pet 2:3; Jud 4; Apoc 17:1; 18:20; 20:4.

against something that is not present to sin against. The New Testament records no such penalty for the failure to recognize the meaning of symbols. *That is because we cannot murder a symbol.*

Either God inspired Paul to impose an unjust penalty upon us (which is impossible), or the Eucharist is the actual Body and Blood of Jesus Christ (which *is* possible). In fact, Paul explains that the reason why some in the Corinthian church had become ill and died was because they received the Eucharist unworthily (1 Cor 11:30). The unworthy reception of Christ's physical body resulted in harmful consequences to their *own* physical bodies. There is a one-to-one correspondence of the effects that Christ's Body had on their bodies, and that is because *both* bodies are present in the reception of Holy Communion. One must ask how a just God could have imposed such harsh penalties upon the Corinthians if they were abusing ordinary bread and wine.

Thus, those who do not discern Christ's body under the appearance of bread and wine bring God's judgment upon them-selves. Paul's use of the word "discerning" the body in v. 29 is from the Greek *diakrino*, which means "to distinguish" or "to sep-arate." For example, James says, "Have you not made *distinctions* among yourselves" relating to rich and poor people (Jas 2:4). Peter similarly says "the Spirit told me to go with them, making no *distinction*" (Acts 11:12), and "he made no *distinction* between us and them," relating to Jews and Gentiles (Acts 15:9).

In these and other cases, the word *diakrino* is used in the con-text of making a distinction between things that are different from each other. As applied here, Paul is commanding the Corinthians to make a distinction between *ordinary* bread and wine and the *consecrated* bread and wine of the Eucharist. If the bread and wine remained bread and wine after the words of con-secration, there would be no "distinctions" to make.

The word *diakrino* can also be associated with "doubting." For example, Jesus tells His apostles to "have faith and never *doubt*" (Mt 21:21). Paul says, "He who has *doubts* is condemned" (Rom 14:23). James says, "Let him ask in faith, with no *doubting*" (Jam 1:6). Jude says, "Convince some, who *doubt*" (v. 22). As applied here, Paul is telling the Corinthians to have *no doubts* about the reality of the Eucharist. What appears to be bread and wine is the actual Body and Blood of the Lord. This mystery is backed up by Jesus' own words, "This is my body; this is my blood," which Paul recounts before issuing his warning.

Uncomfortable with Paul's ominous warning, some Protestants point out that Paul refers to the "bread and cup" in vv. 26 and 27, after he recounts Jesus' use of "body and blood" at the Last Supper in vv. 24 and 25. Thus, they conclude that the "bread and cup" are mere symbols of Christ's "Body and Blood"; otherwise, Paul would not have deliberately switched to using metaphors to describe the "consecrated" elements. There are a number of obvious problems with this analysis.

First, after Paul uses "bread and cup" in vv. 26 and 27, he reverts back to using "body and blood of the Lord" in the same v. 27. In fact, Paul goes back to using "bread and cup" in v. 28 and then uses "body" in v. 29. Paul switches his terminology four times in four verses. We also note that Paul begins his discourse with Jesus' word "body" (v. 24) and ends with the word "body" (v. 29). We have also seen in Scripture how things that have changed are often called what they originally were. Thus, Paul's change in terminology proves nothing for the Protestant apologist.

More importantly, Paul switches back to "body and blood" in v. 27, when he levels his warning about profanation, driving home his point that the "bread and cup" are in fact the "Body and Blood" of Christ and not mere symbols of them. Thus, Paul's purpose in switching back and forth *is to emphasize the distinction between appearance and reality.* What appears to be the "bread and cup" is really the "Body and Blood" of Christ. This is why Paul tells the Corinthians to "discern" (or distinguish) Christ's Body from bread and His Blood from the cup.

Paul's warning brings to mind a debate I had with a Protestant gentleman about the Eucharist. I referred him to the three Synoptic Gospels, where Jesus took bread and wine and said, "This is my body; this is my blood." I pointed out to him that Jesus did not say, "This represents my body" or "This symbolizes my body." I further explained that, because God cannot lie, He cannot declare something to be without making it so. Thus, when God said, "Let there be light," there was light (Gen 1:3). I challenged him to find one case in Scripture where God declared something to be without changing it into what He said it was. He could not.

Instead, my Protestant friend took out a picture of his wife, handed it to me, and said, "This is my wife." He then asked me, "But it is not really her, is it?" He was analogizing his statement "This is my wife" to Jesus' statement "This is my body," in an effort to demonstrate that, just as the picture was a symbol of his wife, the Eucharist is only a symbol of Christ's body. He smiled, thinking he had stumped me.

I smiled back and congratulated him on having such a beautiful wife. I then pretended to rip the picture up, throw it on the floor, stomp all over it, and spit on it. By this time, my friend was looking at me as if I were crazy, so I stopped my act and asked him the key question: "Am I now guilty of your wife's body and blood? After all, I just ripped her up, threw her to the ground, and stomped and spit all over her."

After a long pause, my friend responded "No."

"No," I repeated, "of course not. The picture of your wife is only a symbol of her, and you cannot be guilty of her body and blood by abusing a symbol of her, can you?"

He quickly said, "No, you cannot. That is my point."

"Then," I said, "why does St. Paul, in 1 Corinthians 11:27, tell us we are guilty of Christ's Body and Blood if we receive the Eucharist unworthily? If the Eucharist is just a *symbol* of Christ's Body and Blood, how can we be guilty of a crime against Christ's *actual* Body and Blood by abusing a symbol of it? If the Eucharist is a mere symbol of Christ, like the picture of your wife is a symbol of her, then Paul would be imposing an unjust penalty upon us, would he not?"

My Protestant friend was at a loss for words. He simply asked me to give him back his wife's picture, then told me he would read the verses in their proper context and get back to me. He never did.

Paul's solemn warning to the Corinthians about being guilty of Christ's Body and Blood (literally, murdering Christ) is the most solemn of all warnings in the New Testament. In fact, the New Testament records no other examples of mass-scale sickness and death, such as the Corinthians experienced, for disobeying a divine command.

Paul's dire admonition is certainly a reason why thousands of Christians in the early Church chose martyrdom rather than profane the Eucharist. They chose to die a physical death rather than risk a spiritual death. They chose torture rather than deny the plain words of Jesus and Paul. So, if Protestants truly want to understand what Jesus meant by "This is my body; this is my blood," they need not look any further than Paul's interpretation in 1 Cor 11:27-30.

Actual Participation in Christ's Body and Blood

Paul provides another key teaching on the Eucharist in his first letter to the Corinthians. In chapter 10, Paul reminds the Corinthians of the great miracles that God performed for the Israelites of the Old Testament. He writes about how God led them out of Egypt through the miraculous parting of the Red Sea

(vv. 1-2), how God provided them bread from heaven to eat (v. 3) and water from the rock to drink (v. 4).

In spite of all these miracles, Paul says that God was not pleased with most of them (v. 5). He explains how the Israelites fell into idolatry and sexual immorality, to which God responded by destroying many of them for their sins. Paul tells the Corinthians that these events were written down for our instruction and serve as warnings so that we don't likewise perish (vv. 6,11). After warning them to take heed lest they also fall into idolatry, he says, "I speak as to sensible men; judge for yourselves what I say" (v. 15). He further says:

> The cup of blessing which we bless, is it not a participation in the blood of Christ? The bread which we break, is it not a participation in the body of Christ? Because there is one bread, we who are many are one body, for we all partake of the one bread.
>
> — 1 COR 10:16-17

Thus, Paul makes a neat transition from describing the miracles of the Old Covenant to the miracle of the New Covenant, *the Eucharist.* This comparison is made clear by his consistent warnings after each description. After he describes the miracles of the Old Covenant, he says, "We must not put the Lord to the test" (v. 9). After he describes the Eucharist, he similarly says, "Shall we provoke the Lord to jealousy? Are we stronger than he?" (v. 22).

Why is Paul drawing this parallel? Because he is teaching the Corinthians that in the Eucharist, God performs an even *greater* miracle than He performed for the Jews during the Exodus. In the Eucharist, God does not give His people ordinary bread to sustain them on their earthly journey. Instead, He gives them the Body and Blood of Jesus Christ to sustain them on their heavenly journey. If the Eucharist were just a common meal and not a miracle, Paul would not be comparing it to the incredible miracles of the Old Covenant. He draws this parallel as a solemn reminder to the Corinthians that, through the Eucharist, God has given them a greater gift — but if they sin, He will deliver greater punishments.

Paul's use of the word "participation" (Greek, *koinonia*) also demonstrates that the Eucharist is the Body and Blood of Christ. *Koinonia* means an actual, intimate communion, or sharing, in something else. It does not refer to a symbolic or metaphorical participation. The Corinthians would have certainly understood Paul's usage of the term.

For example, in Paul's second letter to the Corinthians, he uses the same word to describe their nonsacramental civil unions with pagan people:

> Do not be mismated with unbelievers. For what *partnership* have righteousness and iniquity? Or what *fellowship* has light with darkness?
>
> — 2 COR 6:14

Paul uses *koinonia* to describe the actual (not symbolic) one-flesh unions the Corinthians were entering into with unbelievers. Paul uses the same word to describe the Corinthians' actual (not symbolic) one-flesh union with Jesus Christ in the Eucharist.[37]

Paul also phrases his teaching in 1 Cor 10:16 in the form of rhetorical questions: "Is the cup we share not a participation in the blood of Christ? Is the bread we break not a communion with the body of Christ?" Was Paul, the divinely-inspired author, really posing these questions to the Corinthians because he didn't know the answers? Of course not. Paul is employing this technique

---

[37] Paul also uses *koinonia* to describe "sharing" with fellow Christians and calls such sharing a "sacrifice" pleasing to God (Heb 13:15-16). Similarly, John uses *koinonia* to describe the communion Christians have with each other in the context of being cleansed by the "blood of Jesus" (1 Jn 1:7). Paul never uses *koinonia* to describe a mere symbolic communion.

(asking rhetorical questions) to drive home his point and the answer to his questions: *Yes*, the Corinthians are actually sharing in the Body and Blood of Christ.

After explaining the Corinthians' actual participation in the Body and Blood of Christ, Paul focuses on another aspect of the miracle of the Eucharist. He explains that though there are many in the Corinthian church, they all become one body in Christ by partaking of the same bread (v. 17). This would be an odd analysis if the Eucharist were mere common food. Even a husband and wife do not become "one body" by eating a common meal together, but by becoming one flesh in the marital act.

When Paul says that we become one with Christ's *Body*, he means that our union with Christ is physical, not just spiritual. Otherwise, Paul would have called us the "soul of Christ," not the "body of Christ." That is because souls are invisible and spiritual, and bodies are visible and physical. However, our union with Christ can be physical *only* if Christ is actually giving us something physical, that is, Himself. Jesus does this in the Holy Eucharist.

The Eucharist Is a Sacrifice and Meal

After describing the Eucharist as an intimate communion in the Body and Blood of Christ, Paul explains that the Eucharist is both a sacrifice and a meal — *but a sacrifice first*. At the altar, one eats only what is sacrificed. Continuing his warnings to the Corinthians about idolatry, Paul writes:

> Consider the people of Israel; are not those who eat the sacrifices partners in the altar? What do I imply then? That food offered to idols is anything, or that an idol is anything? No, I imply that what pagans sacrifice they offer to demons and not to God. I do not want you to be partners with demons. You cannot drink the cup of the Lord and the cup of demons. You cannot partake of the table of the Lord and the table of demons (vv. 18-21).

In this passage, Paul explains the significance of eating what is offered in sacrifice. When one eats the sacrifice, he becomes a partner (Greek, *koinonos*) with the victim (vv. 18, 20).[38] He shares an intimate, personal communion (*koinonia*) with the one sacrificed. In essence, Paul is saying "you are what you eat." This is why Paul says when we *eat* the Body of Christ, we *become* the Body of Christ. We become Christ's Body because we eat it.

Evidently, the Corinthians were offering both the Eucharistic sacrifice and pagan sacrifices. This explains Paul's repeated warnings about idolatry. He distinguishes the Eucharistic sacrifice from pagan sacrifices by saying "what pagans sacrifice they offer to demons and not to God" (v. 20). In this passage, he is explaining that *both* are sacrifices, but only one is offered to God. Paul's follow-up statement could easily be "what *we* sacrifice, *we* offer to God and not to demons." His issue is not with the sacrifice; his issue is with *what* is being sacrificed and *to whom* it is being offered.

Because Paul uses the phrase "table of the Lord" in v. 21, Protestants attempt to argue that the Eucharist is not a sacrifice. They claim that "tables" are for meals, while "altars" are for sacrifices. This argument overlooks the most obvious fact that Paul uses the word "sacrifice" (from the Greek, *thusia*) three times in four verses. Since the pagans are sacrificing "to demons" in v. 20, and Paul says the Corinthians cannot partake of the "table of demons" in v. 21, this means that the "table" (v. 21) refers to the pagans' place of sacrifice (v. 20). Exegetical consistency (and integrity) requires us to conclude the following:

- Pagans sacrifice to demons; Christians sacrifice to God.
- Pagans offer the cup of demons; Christians offer the cup of the Lord.
- Pagans become partners with demons; Christians become partners with Christ.

---

[38] See also 1 Cor 9:13.

- Pagans offer sacrifice at the table of demons; Christians offer sacrifice at the table of the Lord.

Malachi also uses "table" and "altar" as *synonyms* in the context of offering sacrifice. The prophet uses these terms interchangeably both before and after he prophesies about the eternal sacrifice of the New Covenant (Mal 1:11). Malachi also connects *food* to both the "altar" and "table" because the food is the product of the sacrifice being offered. He writes:

> . . . by offering polluted *food* upon my *altar*. And you say, "How have we polluted it?" By thinking that the LORD's *table* may be despised. When you offer blind animals in *sacrifice*, is that no evil? . . . But you profane it when you say that the LORD's *table* is polluted, and the *food* for it may be despised.[39]

In his letter to the Hebrews, Paul also uses "altar" and "eat" in the context of the New Covenant sacrifice. After spending no less than eleven chapters describing Christ's heavenly priesthood and eternal sacrifice, Paul at the end of his letter writes: "We have an *altar* from which those who serve the tent have no right to *eat*" (Heb 13:10). The Greek word for "altar" (*thusiasterion*) literally means "sacrifice-place" and is the same word Paul uses in the same letter (Hebrews 7:13) to describe the place of the Old Covenant sacrifices. It is also the same word we just saw him use in 1 Cor 10:18 to describe the place of Israel's sacrifices.[40]

Paul is telling us that "we" Christians of the New Covenant have an "altar" of sacrifice, just like the Jews of the Old Covenant did. Those who continue to offer the Old Covenant sacrifices ("those who serve the tent") have no right to eat the New Covenant sacrifice of Christ, for the New has replaced the Old. Because the

---

[39] Mal 1:7-8, 12.

[40] In the New Testament, *thusiasterion* always refers to a place of sacrifice. See, for example, Mt 25:35; Lk 1:11; 11:51; Jas 2:21.

Eucharist is the Body and Blood of Christ offered to God in sacrifice, only those who discern its value have the "right to eat."

Outside of the book of Hebrews, the word "altar" (*thusiasterion*) appears in only one other place in connection with the New Covenant sacrifice: The Apocalypse.[41] This is no surprise because, as we have seen, in the Apocalypse, Jesus appears at the heavenly altar as a sacrificed Lamb (Apoc 5:6). The book provides many allusions to the Eucharistic sacrifice, with references to the priesthood,[42] Christ's Blood,[43] the hidden manna,[44] eating,[45] the temple,[46] and the marriage supper.[47]

In essence, the Apocalypse presents us with a glimpse of the heavenly liturgy. That is why the early Christians incorporated many of the elements of the Apocalypse into their Eucharistic liturgies that are still part of the Catholic Mass today, for example: lamp stands,[48] vestments,[49] incense,[50] a book of God's word,[51] tabernacles,[52] chalices,[53] relics,[54] special prayers,[55] and the Sunday celebration.[56]

[41] Apoc 6:9; 8:3, 5; 9:13; 11:1; 14:18; 16:7.

[42] Apoc 1:6; 4:4, 10; 5:5-6, 8, 11, 14; 7:11, 13; 11:16; 14:3; 19:4.

[43] Apoc 1:5; 5:9; 7:14; 12:11; 19:13.

[44] Apoc 2:17.

[45] Apoc 2:7; 3:20.

[46] Apoc 3:12; 7:15; 11:1-2, 19; 14:15, 17; 15:5-6, 8; 16:1, 17; 21:22.

[47] Apoc 19:9, 17.

[48] Apoc 1:12; 2:5.

[49] Apoc 1:13; 4:4; 6:11; 7:9; 15:6; 19:13-14.

[50] Apoc 5:8; 8:3-4.

[51] Apoc 5:1-2, 5, 9; 6:1, 3, 5, 7, 9, 12; 8:1.

[52] Apoc 11:19; 15:5-6, 8.

[53] Apoc 15:7; 16:1-4, 8, 10, 12, 17; 21:9.

[54] See Apoc 6:9, where the disembodied souls of the saints appear under the heavenly altar, just like the relics of these saints appear under the earthly altars.

[55] See, for example, prayers that follow the *Gloria* (Apoc 15:3-4), the *Alleluia* (19:1, 3-4, 6), the *Holy, Holy, Holy* (4:8), and other antiphonal chants (4:8-11; 5:9-14; 7:10-12; 18:2-8). See also prayers concluding with "Amen" (5:14; 7:12; 19:4).

[56] Apoc 1:10.

Thus, when Paul speaks of us eating from the "altar" in Heb 13:10, he is connecting the earthly liturgy of the Eucharist with the heavenly liturgy of the Apocalypse. This is why, five verses later, he exhorts us to offer the thanksgiving (*eucharistein*) "sacrifice of praise" to God (Heb 10:15). Hebrews speaks of the earthly altar; the Apocalypse speaks of the heavenly altar; but *both* speak of the *same sacrifice* being offered: the one and only New Covenant sacrifice of Jesus Christ. This sacrifice is offered by Christ at the heavenly altar and re-presented by His priests on the earthly altars of the Mass.

In fact, the earthly and heavenly liturgies *are one and the same.* That is because Jesus Christ, our eternal High Priest, is both the one offering and the one being offered. When we celebrate the Eucharistic sacrifice on earth, heaven itself is made present to us, where Christ's Blood speaks to the Father on our behalf. In the Holy Mass, we worship with the angels and saints. We are no longer offering "copies of the heavenly things," but the "sacrifices" of heaven itself (Heb 9:23). Paul explains:

> But you have come to Mount Zion and to the city of the living God, and the heavenly Jerusalem, and to innumerable angels in festal gathering, and to the assembly of the first-born who are enrolled in heaven, and to a judge who is God of all, and to the spirits of just men made perfect, and to Jesus, the mediator of a new covenant, and to the sprinkled blood that speaks more graciously than the blood of Abel. See that you do not refuse him who is speaking.
>
> — HEB 12:22-25

Paul connects this festal gathering to Mount Zion, where Jesus established the Eucharistic sacrifice and which was miraculously preserved after the destruction of the Temple in Jerusalem.[57] John in the Apocalypse also connects the Lamb's heavenly liturgy to

---

[57] See Ps 2:6; 20:2-3; 132:13.

Mount Zion (Apoc 14:1). If one neglects to "meet together" to celebrate the heavenly Eucharist, he "has spurned the Son of God, and profaned the blood of the covenant by which he was sanctified, and outraged the Spirit of grace" (Heb 10:29).[58]

Because we offer the sacrifice of the Lamb, we must also eat the sacrificed Lamb. Paul tells us:

> For Christ, our paschal lamb, has been sacrificed. Let us, therefore, *celebrate the festival*, not with the old leaven, the leaven of malice and evil, but with the unleavened bread of sincerity and truth.[59]

Paul's directive to consume the Eucharistic sacrifice follows the pattern of the Levitical sacrifices, where the animal was killed and eaten. The killing of the animal made atonement for sin, and the eating of the animal restored communion with God. In consecrating His Old Covenant priests, God commanded:

> "They shall eat those things with which atonement was made, to ordain and consecrate them, but an outsider shall not eat of them, because they are holy."
>
> — Ex 29:33

The consummation of the sacrifice symbolized the covenant bond that God had with His people. For example, the Mosaic covenant was consummated with a meal in the presence of God (Ex 24:9-11). The Aaronic sacrifices also had to be consumed.[60] We further remember how God saved Abraham's firstborn son on Mt. Moriah with a substitute sacrifice that had to be consumed (Gen

---

[58] This is why the Catholic Church requires Catholics to attend Sunday Mass and other Holy Days of Obligation under pain of mortal sin.

[59] 1 Cor 5:7-8. In the Passover Seder meal, unleavened bread was used. By commanding us to eat the new "unleavened bread," Paul is telling us that the Eucharist is the new Passover sacrifice, in which the Lamb is slain and consumed.

[60] See, for example, Ex 29:32; Lev 6:16, 26, 29; 7:16; 10:12-14; 19:6; 24:9.

22:9-13). God would later offer His firstborn Son on a hill on that same Mt. Moriah, a sacrifice that must also be consumed.

The most important sacrifice and meal that prefigured the Eucharistic sacrifice and meal was that of the Passover lamb. We read about the institution of the Passover in the twelfth chapter of Exodus. To commemorate Israel's exodus from slavery in Egypt, God required each family to sacrifice a lamb (12:6). The lamb had to be without blemish (12: 5), and not a bone of the lamb could be broken.[61] Further, the people had to sprinkle the blood of the lamb on their doorposts with hyssop.[62] When God came through the land of Egypt that evening and saw the blood, He would "pass over" those homes and spare the families of His wrath.

However, God required more than just the sacrifice and sprinkled blood. He commanded the Israelites to eat the flesh of the sacrificed lamb. The lamb was slaughtered, roasted, and eaten to atone for sin and restore covenant communion with God.[63] If God's people sacrificed the lamb but did not eat it, He would slay their firstborn sons (v. 12).[64]

We also note that no one outside of God's covenant could eat the lamb (v. 43). This corresponds to the Catholic Church's requirement that one must be a member of the Church to receive the Eucharist. Receiving Holy Communion means one is in communion with Jesus Christ *and* His Church, because the Church is His Mystical Body.

Also, no uncircumcised person could eat the lamb (v. 48). Since Baptism is the "circumcision" of the New Covenant,[65] this

---

[61] Ex 12:46; Num 9:12.

[62] Ex 12:7, 22-23.

[63] Ex 12:8, 11, 46; 2 Chron 30:15-17; 35:1, 6, 11, 13; Ezek 6:20-21.

[64] After God freed His people from the slavery of Egypt, He sustained them on their journey to the Promised Land with bread from heaven (Ex 6:4-36; Neh 9:15). This manna from heaven foreshadowed the true bread from heaven, Jesus Christ (see Ps 78:24-25; 105:40; 2 Kings 4:43; see also Wis 16:20; Sir 24:21).

[65] Col 2:11-12.

corresponds to the Church's requirement that one must be baptized to receive the Eucharist. In light of Paul's solemn warning in 1 Cor 11:27, the Church wants to ensure that the Eucharist is received only by those who appreciate its worth, lest they be "guilty of the body and blood of the Lord."

Requiring non-Catholics to make preparations to receive the Eucharist (Baptism, catechesis) is the same reason why the Church requires couples to be married before having conjugal relations. A man and a woman cannot experience the blessings of the one-flesh union until they are in a covenant relationship with each other (called the sacrament of Marriage). Similarly, one cannot experience the grace of the one-flesh union with Jesus in the Eucharist until the person is in a covenant relationship with Him (called the sacrament of Baptism).

In recording Jesus' Passion, the Apostle John conspicuously connects Jesus' sacrifice with the sacrifice of the Passover lambs. For example, when Jesus is arrested, John points out that Pilate found no blemish or fault in Him.[66] This happened at the same time the lambs were being examined for blemishes before being sacrificed (Jn 19:14). John tells us that Jesus had on a priestly tunic which had no seam, woven from top to bottom (Jn 19:23). This was the same *chiton* garment the Old Testament priests wore to offer sacrifices.[67] John also tells us that Jesus was provided wine on a hyssop branch, the same kind of branch used to sprinkle the Passover lambs' blood on the doorposts (Jn 19:29). Finally, John records that none of Jesus' bones were broken, just like the Passover lambs' bones could not be broken.[68]

---

[66] Jn 18:39; 19:4, 6. See also Lk 23:4, 14; Heb 9:14.

[67] See Ex 28:4; Lev 16:4. This demonstrates that Jesus is both Priest and Victim.

[68] Jn 19:33, 36. After Jesus died and the soldier pierced His side with a lance, John records that "at once there came out blood and water" (Jn 19:34). The Church views the blood as a symbol of the Eucharist and the water as a symbol of Baptism, without which one cannot receive the Eucharist.

What does this mean? It means that we must eat our New Covenant Passover Lamb, just as God commanded in the Old Covenant. Just as the Old Covenant Passover was a sacrifice and a meal, the Eucharist is also a sacrifice and a meal. Jesus tells us to "take and eat," and Paul tells us to "celebrate the feast." The Old Passover memorialized the Jews' freedom from the slavery of Egypt, while the New Passover celebrates the Christians' freedom from the slavery of sin. Just as the people of the Old Covenant ate bread from heaven on their journey to the promised land of Canaan, those of the New Covenant eat the true bread from heaven on their journey to true Promised Land — heaven itself.

Jesus' command that we must eat His flesh and drink His blood is the most powerful and scandalous of all His teachings. We now examine the Master's teaching in detail as recorded in the Gospel of John.

"WHOEVER EATS MY FLESH AND DRINKS MY BLOOD . . ."

In chapter 6 of John's Gospel, Jesus gives us His definitive teaching on the Eucharist. As we will see, while in a synagogue in Capernaum, Jesus told His disciples that they must eat His flesh and drink His blood to have eternal life. Jesus presented His teaching on the Eucharist about a year before His Passion. Thus, the Gospel of John records Jesus' promise of the Eucharist, and the Synoptic Gospels record His fulfillment of the promise at the Last Supper.

We should note that a major theme of John's Gospel is the Incarnation. Unlike the Synoptic Gospels, which begin by focusing on Jesus' human nature, John opens His Gospel by emphasizing Jesus' divine nature: "In the beginning was the Word, and the Word was with God, and the *Word was God* . . . And the *Word became flesh* and dwelt among us."[69] Five chapters later, Jesus will tell us that we must eat that very flesh.

Because the Eucharist is an extension of the Incarnation, it is no surprise that John leads us into Jesus' teaching on the Eucharist by first establishing His divinity. After all, eating ordinary human flesh avails nothing; it is the divine flesh of the Son of God that gives life (Jn 6:63). We must first believe in the Incarnation before we can believe in the Eucharist. John establishes Jesus' divinity by recording two of His miracles (vv. 1-34). We might call this Phase One of John's presentation.

In Phase Two, John records Jesus' Eucharistic discourse (vv. 35-71). Phase Two is composed of two parts: (a) that we must have personal *faith* in Jesus as the Son of God; and, (b) that we must put that faith into *action* by consuming His flesh and blood. We must not merely accept Jesus as personal Lord and Savior, but do what He commands no matter how incredible it seems. We must believe in the person of Jesus before we can share an intimate, covenant relationship with Him. By establishing Jesus' divinity through miracles, John assures us that we can have faith that He is the Son of God. Because He is the Son of God, He can give us His flesh and blood to eat, a very sharing in His Incarnation.

Phase One — Jesus' Divinity

John begins chapter 6 by recording Jesus' miracle of the multiplication of the loaves. At the sea of Tiberius, while the feast of the Passover was at hand, Jesus was surrounded by thousands of hungry people who were following Him. Wishing to feed the multitude but only having five barley loaves and two fish, Jesus

---

[69] Jn 1:1, 14. Jesus was born in the city of "Bethlehem" (Mt 2:1; Lk 2:4), which means "house of bread." Scripture also says Mary laid Jesus in a "manger," (Lk 2:7,12,16) which is a place where animals "eat." If not coincidental, these facts further point to Jesus as "bread" which must be "eaten."

"took the loaves, and when he had given thanks, he distributed them to those who were seated; so also the fish, as much as they wanted" (6:11). After the people were fed, Jesus commanded His apostles to gather up the fragments which amounted to twelve baskets (vv. 12-13). When the people experienced the miracle, they said, "This is indeed the prophet who is to come into the world!" (v. 14).

Jesus' miracle establishes His divine power, in which the same people will need to believe when they hear His teachings on the Eucharist. In fact, the miracle is symbolic of the Eucharist, which Jesus is about to reveal. Jesus "gave thanks" before performing the miracle of multiplication, just like He "gave thanks" before performing the miracle of transubstantiation.[70] The multiplied, unconsumed bread that remained after the miracle is symbolic of Jesus remaining with His disciples in the Eucharist even after His Ascension into heaven.[71]

Thereafter, Jesus and His apostles got into a boat and traveled across the sea to Capernaum. When it became dark and windy, the apostles "saw Jesus walking on the sea and drawing near the boat" (v. 19). When they saw Jesus defying the laws of physics, the apostles became terrified. But Jesus said, "It is I; do not be afraid" (v. 20). Then the apostles took Jesus into the boat, and immediately the boat arrived at their destination (v. 21). In this account, Jesus is demonstrating His divinity exclusively to His apostles. They will need complete faith in His divinity to accept His teaching on the Eucharist and implement His teaching as priests of the New Covenant. If they have faith, they and their fellow Christians will reach their eternal destination.

---

[70] See also verse 23.

[71] Jesus may also have been alluding to His Eucharistic presence among us after His Ascension when He says, "Wherever the body is, there the eagles will be gathered together" (Mt 24:28).

At this point, the crowds who witnessed the multiplication of the loaves seek to find Jesus. When they find Him, Jesus rebukes their unbelief by saying:

> "Truly, truly, I say to you, you seek me, not because you saw signs, but because you ate your fill of the loaves. Do not labor for the food that perishes, but for the food which endures to eternal life, which the Son of man will give to you."
>
> (vv. 26-27)

Jesus is telling the crowds that they believe in Him because He filled their bellies with earthly food, but such passing faith is not good enough. Soon He will tell them that they will have to eat a different kind of food, namely His flesh and blood, and that will require faith of a different degree. When the crowd asks what kind of "works" they must do, Jesus emphasizes what God requires in the New Covenant: "This is the work of God, that you *believe* in him whom he has sent" (v. 29).

At this point, taking pride in their heritage, the people remind Jesus that God did works for their ancestors during the exodus by giving them manna in the desert to eat (v. 31). Since Jesus was putting the onus of *belief* on them, they in turn put the onus of *works* on Jesus (remember, the Jews were basing their relationship with God on works, not faith). They ask Him, "What work do *you* perform?" (v. 30).

Jesus sets the stage for His discourse on the Eucharist by responding, "Truly, truly, I say to you, it was not Moses who gave you the bread from heaven; my Father gives you the true bread from heaven. For the bread of God is that which comes down from heaven, and gives life to the world" (v. 32-33). And they said, "Lord, give us this bread always" (v. 34). From here, Jesus transitions into His Eucharistic discourse. He will first require New Covenant *faith* in Him, and later, *action* to demonstrate that faith.

Phase Two — Jesus' Eucharistic Discourse

John provides two markers to highlight the two parts of Jesus' discourse. These two markers are Jesus' statement, "I am the bread of life." Jesus says this about Himself in v. 35 to mark the first part (faith), and again in v. 48 to mark the second part (action). Let's examine these parts in detail.

a. Faith

After Jesus calls Himself the "bread of life," He says "he who comes to me shall not hunger, and he who *believes* in me shall never thirst. But I said to you that you have seen me and yet do not *believe*" (vv. 35-36). At this initial stage, Jesus' goal is to emphasize the importance of having personal faith in Him. The people need to believe in Him before they can respond to His teachings. He points out their lack of faith for the following reason: if they have already "seen" Him and His miracle of the loaves and still do not believe in Him, they will never believe what He is about to teach them about the Eucharist.

Many Protestants want to equate Jesus' use of "bread" in v. 35 as a metaphor for the personal faith Jesus requires. If "bread" is a metaphor for belief in v. 35, then the Protestant can maintain his metaphorical interpretation of "bread" throughout the rest of Jesus' discourse. This is a faulty hermeneutic for a number of reasons.[72]

---

[72] We should note that Catholics, like Protestants, also believe in a symbolic interpretation of Jn 6. For example, when Jesus says He is "the bread of life," there is a symbolic and spiritual dimension to Jesus' teaching. It is erroneous, however, to advance the spiritual interpretation *at the exclusion* of the literal interpretation. Most of the errors in Protestant theology stem from this flawed hermeneutic. Sound biblical exegesis requires us to interpret the Scriptures in their literal and obvious sense, unless the interpretation is untenable or necessity requires otherwise. As we will plainly see in this section, a literal interpretation of Jn 6 predominates over a symbolic one.

First, v. 35 must be interpreted in the context of the entire sixth chapter of John's Gospel, which we are doing here. Second, Jesus' use of "bread" refers to himself, while His use of "belief" refers to His disciples. Jesus does not equate "bread" with "belief," but that His disciples must *believe* that *He* is the bread from heaven. Third, as we mentioned and will further see below, Jesus says He is the "bread" from heaven in v. 48 as well, which kicks off His explanation of what His disciples must do with that "bread" (eat it).

As Jesus speaks about the need to have faith, He also incorporates into His teaching the mystery of grace. As we have seen, *faith* leads to the *grace* of the New Covenant, and the foundation of the New Covenant is the Eucharist. Thus, Jesus' teachings on grace are perfectly appropriate at this juncture. He says, "All that the Father gives me will come to me; and him who comes to me I will not cast out" (v. 37); "this is the will of him who sent me, that I should lose nothing of all that he has given me, but raise it up at the last day" (v. 39); "For this is the will of my Father, that every one who sees the Son and believes in him should have eternal life; and I will raise him up at the last day" (v. 40).

In these verses, Jesus is speaking of God's grace and how a person must respond to that grace by his free will. Jesus makes this clear when He says, "No one can come to me *unless the Father who sent me draws him;* and I will raise him up at the last day" (v. 44). Because the Father wills that none be lost (v. 39), He makes the first move by drawing the person with His grace (v. 44). The person that is drawn must respond to the grace by "coming" to Jesus (v. 37) and "believing" in Him (v. 40).

Because Jesus says "who comes to me I will not cast out" (v. 37) and that "I should lose nothing" of those the Father gives Him (v. 39), some Protestants conclude that Jesus is teaching about eternal security. But Jesus is teaching nothing of the sort. Jesus will not cast out the one who comes to Him, but there is no guarantee the person *will* come, nor any guarantee he will *stay* if he comes.

While the Father's will is that Jesus "should lose nothing" of those who the Father gives Him, there is no assurance the person will remain with Jesus after the Father's giving. This is why Jesus says "he who endures to the end will be saved."[73] Moreover, the Father "gives" to Jesus only those who freely respond to His drawing. These points are demonstrated elsewhere in John's Gospel.

For example, Jesus tells the Jews "yet you *refuse* to come to me that you may have life" (Jn 5:40). In this verse, Jesus emphasizes the free-will side of the equation. The Father was drawing the Jews with His grace, but they refused to respond to His drawing. Jesus also says, "I, when I am lifted up from the earth, will draw all men to myself" (Jn 12:40). Because all men don't eventually come to Jesus or stay with Jesus, free will must be part of the drawing process. James says, "Draw near to God and he will draw near to you" (4:8). These verses explain that there is a dynamic between God's grace and human free-will decisions. God, as Prime Mover, draws us by His grace, but we must respond to that grace to be saved. The common Protestant's error occurs when he emphasizes the grace side of the equation at the exclusion of the free-will side.[74]

At the conclusion of this first part of Phase Two, Jesus emphasizes that His teaching comes directly from God. In quoting the prophet Isaiah, Jesus says, "And they shall all be taught by God" (v. 45).[75] Jesus' teaching comes from God, *because He is God*. About Himself, Jesus says, "Not that any one has seen the

---

[73] Mt 10:22; 24:13; Mk 13:13.

[74] God always makes the first move by providing man grace that moves the man's mind toward God. If the man doesn't resist the grace (Acts 7:51; Jn 5:40; 2 Cor 6:1), then God assists the man with the grace by strengthening his will and making him capable of acting (Phil 2:13; 2 Cor 3:5). Thus, there are two effects from the same grace, which Aquinas calls "operating" grace (God operates so that we can will good) and "cooperating" grace (God cooperates with the will so we can work good). Thus, Paul says, "God is at work in you, both *to will* and *to work* for his good pleasure" (Phil 2:13).

[75] See Is 54:13.

Father except him who is from God; he has seen the Father. Truly, truly, I say to you, he who believes has eternal life" (vv. 46-47). Thus, as Jesus transitions into the next part of His teaching, He wants the people know He is God in the flesh. Only if they accept the mystery of *His divinity* will they be able to accept the mystery of the Eucharist.

b. Action

As we have already mentioned, Jesus begins this second section of Phase Two by repeating, "I am the bread of life" (v. 48). Jesus reminds the Jews that their ancestors ate the manna in the wilderness and still died, and that He is not talking about that kind of bread. Now, for the first time, Jesus introduces four new aspects of His teaching: that we must *act* on our faith by *eating* the bread, that it is a *living* bread, that He will *give* the bread, and that this bread is really His *flesh*. He says, "I am the living bread which came down from heaven; if any one eats this bread, he will live forever; and the bread which I shall give for the life of the world is my flesh" (v. 51).[76]

When Jesus said "eat" this bread in v. 51, John uses the Greek *phago* for "eat." *Phago* is used 97 times in the New Testament, and it always refers to physically eating food, with only one nominal exception.[77] Because *phago* refers to eating food, the Jews imme-

---

[76] Because Jesus had not yet instituted the Eucharist, He uses the verb "give" in the future tense: ". . . which I *shall give* (Greek, *didomi*) for the life of the world" (v. 51). At the Last Supper, Jesus fulfills the promise by using "give" in the present tense: "This is my body which *is given* (Greek, *didomenon*) for you" (Lk 22:19). There is a clear connection between the promise of the Eucharist in Jn 6 and the institution of the Eucharist in the Gospels.

[77] See Jn 4:32-34. This exception actually incorporates, not excludes, Jesus' literal use of *phago* two chapters later. When Jesus says He has food to "eat" and this "food is to do the *will*" of the Father in Jn 4, He repeats this theme in Jn 6: "This is the *will* of him who sent me" (v. 39), and "This is the *will* of my Father" (v. 40). Jn 6 is not only about believing, but about physically eating the bread from heaven.

diately object to Jesus' teaching. They ask, "How can this man give us his flesh to eat?" (v. 52). Thus, the Jews understood Jesus to be speaking literally about eating His flesh. If Jesus wanted to be understood figuratively and not literally, it would have been His duty not only as the Son of God but as an honest teacher to correct the Jews and say to them: "You misunderstood me. I was not speaking of literally eating my flesh. I was speaking only metaphorically about believing in me."

Did Jesus correct the Jews? Did He tell them that their literal interpretation was way off base? Far from it. Instead, Jesus responds to their objection by using a double expletive ("Truly, truly") which corresponds to an oath, and then gives them an even more explicit teaching about literally eating His flesh:

> "Truly, truly, I say to you, unless you eat the flesh of the Son of man and drink his blood, you have no life in you; he who eats my flesh and drinks my blood has eternal life, and I will raise him up at the last day. For my flesh is food indeed and my blood is drink indeed. He who eats my flesh and drinks my blood abides in me, and I in him. As the living Father sent me, and I live because of the Father, so he who eats me will live because of me. This is the bread which came down from heaven, not such as the fathers ate and died; he who eats this bread will live forever."
>
> (vv. 53-58)

Jesus Switches to a Stronger Word for "Eat"

Jesus' foregoing dissertation is among the most powerful in Sacred Scripture. As He emphasizes the "action" part of His teaching, Jesus increases the literalness of His message in vv. 53-58 in a number of dramatic ways. First, Jesus changes the verb for "eat" which eliminates the possibility that He is speaking metaphorically. Before, in vv. 49-51, John uses *phago* three times:

once to describe physically "eating" the manna in the desert; and the other two times to describe "eating" Jesus' living bread.[78]

Now, in vv. 54 and 56-58, John uses an even stronger verb, *trogo*, four times to describe "eating" Jesus' flesh. *Trogo* means to chew, gnaw, nibble, or crunch. It is used only two other times in the New Testament, and exclusively in reference to the literal mastication of food.[79] It is never used metaphorically. There is simply no reason for Jesus to switch from *phago* to *trogo* unless He wanted to confirm the Jews' suspicion that they must literally eat His flesh (or mislead the entire early Church into the grossest of all errors). We also note that the Jews understood Jesus literally, even *before* He switched from *phago* to *trogo*, when they asked: "How can this man give us his flesh to eat (*phago*)?" (v. 52). Thus, Jesus switched to a stronger verb *in response* to the Jews' objection.

To further bolster the literal interpretation of His teaching, Jesus says, "For my flesh is food *indeed* and my blood is drink *indeed*" (v. 55). The Greek word for "indeed" is the adjective *alethes* which means "true," "truly," or "truth." It is used 24 other times in the New Testament and is *always* connected to object nouns that are literal, not metaphorical.[80] In fact, *alethes* is used

---

[78] We can analogize Jesus' command to "eat" in Jn 6 to God's command to "not eat" in the Garden of Eden (Gen 2:17). Both commands dealt with literal, not symbolic, eating. When Adam "ate" in the Garden, he brought death to himself. When we "eat" of the food of the Second Adam, we bring life to ourselves.

[79] Jesus uses *trogo* to describe how the people "were *eating* and drinking, marrying and giving in marriage" before the flood (Mt 24:38). In reference to Judas, Jesus also says, "He who *ate* my bread has lifted his heel against me" (Jn 13:18). In both instances *trogo* refers to literally (not symbolically) eating food.

[80] Mt 22:16; Mk 12:14; Jn 3:33; 4:18; 5:31-32; 7:18; 8:13-14, 16-17; 10:41; 19:35; 21:24; Acts 12:9; Rom 3:4; 2 Cor 6:8; Phil 4:8; Titus 1:3; 1 Pet 5:12; 2 Pet 2:22; 1 Jn 2:8, 27; 3 Jn 1:12. The Greek makes the connection very strong: "flesh of me true is food" (*sarx mou alethes estin brosis*); "blood of me true is drink" (*haima mou alethes estin posis*).

most often in Scripture *to validate oral or written statements.*[81] Thus, the use of *alethes* in v. 55 is responsive to those who had doubts about Jesus' oral teaching that His flesh and blood were really food and drink. Jesus essentially responds by saying, "Yes, you understood my statement correctly; my flesh is *true* food and blood *true* drink." Remember, Jesus' use of "true" to describe His flesh and blood is coming from the Truth Himself (Jn 14:6).

Note that Jesus says if we don't consume His flesh and blood, we have "no *life*" in us (v. 53); but if we do, we will have "eternal *life*" (v. 54) and will "*live*" forever" (v. 58). Jesus' repeated references to "life" point to the intimate, covenant communion that He gives us in the Holy Eucharist. Similar to a husband and wife who give life in their one-flesh union in the sacrament of Marriage, Jesus gives us life in our one-flesh union with Him in the sacrament of the Eucharist.[82]

For those who eat His flesh and drink His blood, Jesus says, "I will raise him up at the last day" (v. 54).[83] Jesus connects the Eucharist with the Resurrection at the Second Coming. Just as we eat Jesus' actual flesh in the Eucharist, He will raise our actual flesh on the last day. Because Jesus comes to judge us on the last day, the Eucharist is a type of Second Coming and Judgment as well. Christ comes to us sacramentally in the Eucharist, until He

---

[81] Mt 22:16; Mk 12:14; Jn 3:33; 8:16-17, 26; 10:41; 19:35; 21:24; Titus 1:3; 1 Pet 5:12; 1 Jn 2:27; 3 Jn 1:12.

[82] We draw this comparison only to emphasize that the heart of "sacrament" is covenant renewal. We do not mean to equate the marital act (a natural good) with the reception of the Eucharist (a supernatural good), as some modern theologians do. In fact, Scripture teaches that holiness is best achieved by *suppressing* carnal desires (1 Cor 7:1,7), as there are no marriages or carnal relations in heaven (Mt 22:30; Mk 12:25). Attempting to explain the supernatural by means of the natural is an error called Reductionism.

[83] Jesus refers to raising us up at the "last day" in verses 39-40, 44 as well. The phrase "last day" appears only in John's Gospel, also in 7:37 (in reference to feasting in heaven); 11:24 (resurrection); and 12:48 (the Final Judgment). See also 2 Tim 1:18, where Paul refers to "that day" as the Day of Judgment of the dead.

comes again at the Parousia (1 Cor 11:26). Further, He judges our worthiness to receive Him which brings us either grace and salvation or judgment and damnation (1 Cor 11:29).

While Protestants contend that Jesus' use of "flesh and blood" refer only to His sacrifice on the Cross, there is absolutely no exegetical basis for such an interpretation. Certainly, Christ gave up His flesh and blood on the Cross. But Jesus never mentions the Cross in Jn 6. Moreover, there is no passage in Scripture that equates eating Christ's flesh with the Atonement, nor is there any passage that tells us to symbolically consume Christ's flesh and blood to attain eternal life. Scripture never even refers to eating flesh or drinking blood as a metaphor for belief.[84] That, coupled with Jesus' use of *trogo* and *alethes*, which are never used metaphorically, compels any honest Christian to conclude that Jesus was speaking literally, just as everyone understood Him.

Jesus Uses the Word "Flesh"

Jesus' introduction of His "flesh" is another significant change in His discourse that increases the literal meaning of His message. Before, in vv. 48 and 50-51, Jesus only mentioned the "bread" that He will give. Now, in vv. 51 and 53-56, Jesus says that the bread He will give is His flesh. Jesus' change in terminology certainly got the Jews' attention because they based their objection on His use of "flesh," not "bread," when they said, "How can this man give us His *flesh* to eat?" (v. 52). Just as Jesus switches from *phago* (eat) to *trogo* (chew), He uses *sarx* (flesh), not *soma* (body), to make His point unmistakably clear. By using the most literal terminology possible, Jesus put the meaning of His message beyond dispute.

---

[84] In addition to the complete absence of biblical precedent for the Protestant position, we also note that bread and wine are not — either by their nature or as a figure of speech — symbols for flesh and blood.

Some Protestant apologists correctly point out that Jesus used *soma*, not *sarx*, in His institution of the Eucharist: "This is my *body* (*soma*)." Because Jesus uses *sarx* in Jn 6, the Protestant concludes that there is no connection between Jesus' teaching in Jn 6 and the Last Supper. This argument ignores the fact that Jesus used *haima* (blood) in both Jn 6 and at the Last Supper. That these were the only two times Jesus referred to giving His Blood to drink necessarily connects the two events. In Jn 6, Jesus promised to give us His Blood to drink; at the Last Supper, Jesus actually gave His Blood to drink.

Ironically, to argue that there is no connection between Jn 6 and the Last Supper backfires on the Protestant because Jesus' language in Jn 6 and the Last Supper is *either* literal *or* symbolic. It is one or the other. If there is no connection between the two, then the language in one must be literal and the other symbolic. The Protestant cannot successfully argue that Jesus' language in both Jn 6 and the Last Supper are symbolic, and yet claim that there is no connection between them. This shows the internal inconsistency of the argument.

The Protestant argument also overlooks the fact that *sarx* and *soma* are synonyms for the human body. Thus, they are used interchangeably in Scripture. For example:

- Who will deliver me from this body (*soma*) of death? Thanks be to God through Jesus Christ our Lord! So then, I of myself serve the law of God with my mind, but with my flesh (*sarx*) I serve the law of sin.

  — ROM 7:24-25

- . . . for if you live according to the flesh (*sarx*) you will die, but if by the Spirit you put to death the deeds of the body (*soma*) you will live.

  — ROM 8:13

- Do you not know that he who joins himself to a prostitute becomes one body (*soma*) with her? For, as it is written, "The two shall become one flesh (*sarx*)."

  — 1 COR 6:16

- . . . always carrying in the body (*soma*) the death of Jesus, so that the life of Jesus may also be manifested in our bodies (*soma*). For while we live we are always being given up to death for Jesus' sake, so that the life of Jesus may be manifested in our mortal flesh (*sarx*).

  — 2 COR 4:10-11

- For no man ever hates his own flesh (*sarx*), but nourishes and cherishes it, as Christ does the church, because we are members of his body (*soma*).

  — EPH 5:29-30

- These have indeed an appearance of wisdom in promoting rigor of devotion and self-abasement and severity to the body (*soma*), but they are of no value in checking the indulgence of the flesh (*sarx*).

  — COL 2:23

Because *sarx* and *soma* refer to the human body, there is no significant basis to differentiate Jesus' use of the terms in Jn 6 and at the Last Supper. In both cases, Jesus is referring *to the flesh of His Body*. As with His Blood, that Jesus refers to giving His Body to eat *only* in Jn 6 and the Last Supper connects the events beyond question. Because Jesus in Jn 6 is introducing the Eucharist for the very first time, He chose the most literal words possible. Jesus chose the most literal words to provide the theological foundation His apostles would later need to understand the real meaning of His words at the Last Supper: "Take and eat; this is my body."

Arguing that Jesus used *sarx* only symbolically poses another major problem for the Protestant apologist. In fact, it is the fatal blow to the Protestant position. Whenever "eating flesh" and "drinking blood" are used figuratively in the Scriptures, it always refers to attacking or destroying an enemy, not becoming intimately close with a friend. For example:

In describing how God allowed Israel to be invaded by enemies, Isaiah writes:

> They snatch on the right, but are still hungry, and they devour on the left, but are not satisfied; each devours his neighbor's flesh . . .
>
> — Is 9:20

God would reverse Israel's fortunes if she would turn back to Him:

> However, I will make your oppressors *eat their own flesh, and they shall be drunk with their own blood as with wine.* Then all flesh shall know that I am the LORD your Savior, and your Redeemer, the Mighty One of Jacob.
>
> — Is 49:26

God similarly says:

> Now it shall be said of Jacob and Israel, "What has God wrought! Behold, a people! As a lioness it rises up and as a lion it lifts itself; it does not lie down *till it devours the prey, and drinks the blood of the slain."*
>
> — NUM 23:23-24

When God issued His judgment against the nation of Gog, He revealed it to Ezekiel:

> "Assemble and come, gather from all sides to the sacrificial feast which I am preparing for you, a great sacrificial feast upon the mountains of Israel, and you shall eat flesh and drink blood. You shall eat the flesh of the mighty, and

drink the blood of the princes of the earth . . . And you shall eat fat till you are filled, and drink blood till you are drunk . . . And you shall be filled at my table with horses and riders, with mighty men and all kinds of warriors," says the Lord GOD.

— EZEK 39:17-20

God condemned the evil rulers of Israel who treated their own people like enemies when He said:

"You who hate the good and love the evil, who tear the skin from off my people, and their flesh from off their bones; *who eat the flesh of my people*, and flay their skin from off them . . ."

— MIC 3:2-3

We also see this figurative language in the Apocalypse to describe the attacks of God's enemies. For example:

- "Just art thou in these thy judgments, thou who art and wast, O Holy One. For men have shed the blood of saints and prophets, and *thou hast given them blood to drink*" (Apoc 16:5-6).
- "Babylon the great, mother of harlots and of earth's abominations." And I saw the woman, *drunk with the blood of the saints and the blood of the martyrs of Jesus* (Apoc 17:5-6).
- "They and the beast will hate the harlot; they will make her desolate and naked, and *devour her flesh* and burn her up with fire" (Apoc 17:16).

Eating flesh and drinking blood, when used figuratively in the Scriptures, invariably refers to assaulting or destroying an enemy. It never has any positive connotations. Thus, if Jesus were really speaking figuratively in Jn 6, He would be saying, "He who assaults me has eternal life." Such an interpretation does not dignify a rebuttal. The impossibility of applying a figurative meaning to Jn 6 forces us to interpret Jesus' words literally, just as His audience and the entire early Church did.

Jesus Adds That We Must "Drink His Blood"

Jesus' command that we also "drink His Blood" is another dramatic shift in His presentation. We again recall that, in vv. 48-51, Jesus tells His disciples that He is the living bread come down from heaven, that they must eat this bread to live forever, and that the bread is really His flesh. Jesus says nothing about drinking His Blood in those verses. It is only *after* the Jews object to eating His flesh that Jesus issues the command to drink His Blood. He issues the command three separate times (vv. 53-54, 56) confirming for His audience that His Blood is "real drink" indeed (v. 55). As with His verb change for "eat" (*phago* to *trogo*), Jesus adds the blood-drinking requirement to eliminate any doubt that He is speaking literally.

Jesus' command to drink His Blood was repulsive to the Jews. Under the Old Covenant, God forbade the Jews from consuming blood because blood was considered a source of life: "Only you shall not eat flesh with its life, that is, its blood" (Gen 9:4); "Whoever eats any blood, that person shall be cut off from his people" (Lev 7:27).[85] On the basis of these Old Covenant prohibitions, Protestants argue that Jesus could not have literally given His Blood to drink as the source of life in the New Covenant. This argument is easily refuted.

Most obviously, the laws of the Old Covenant have been superseded by the laws of the New Covenant.[86] All of the Jewish religious laws and rituals concerning festivals, diets, circumcision, and consuming blood are obsolete. While the Church at the council of Jerusalem recommended that the Gentiles abstain

---

[85] See also Lev 3:17; 7:25-26; 17:11-14; Deut 12:16, 23-24.
[86] 2 Cor 3:14; Heb 7:18; 8:7; 10:9.

from consuming blood and food strangled or offered to idols, this was a temporary, pastoral decision made to facilitate the Jews' inclusion in the Church.[87] Paul made it clear that this was not a dogmatic decision by permitting these practices if they didn't harm the conscience of a fellow believer.[88]

Moreover, the Old Covenant proscribed drinking literal blood from dead animals. This has nothing to do with drinking the living Bood of Jesus Christ. In the Eucharist, we drink the Blood of the risen Jesus under the sacramental appearance of wine. Thus, there is not a one-to-one correspondence between the blood of the Old and New Covenants. We also remember that the Old Covenant was not designed to give life, only knowledge of sin. Because blood was the source of life, it could not be drunk. In the New Covenant, the very blood that removes the Old Covenant laws now actually gives life, and must be drunk.

Because God's people are no longer under the dietary restrictions of the Mosaic law but live in the freedom of Christ, Paul can say, "the kingdom of God is not food and drink but righteousness and peace and joy in the Holy Spirit" (Rom 14:17). "Therefore," Paul says, "let no one pass judgment on you in questions of food and drink or with regard to a festival or a new moon or a Sabbath" (Col 2:16).

"This Is a Hard Saying; Who Can Listen to It?"

After the disciples listen to Jesus' teaching, they are utterly scandalized. Just as they objected eight verses earlier when they said, "How can this man give us His flesh to eat?" (v. 52), they now issue their second objection: "This is a hard saying; who can listen to it?" (v. 60). The disciples don't even want to *listen* to Jesus' graphic words, much less understand the meaning of them.

---

[87] See Acts 15:28-29; 21:25.
[88] 1 Cor 8:1-13; Rom 14:14-18; 1 Tim 4:3.

Just as we see a crescendo in the explicitness of Jesus' teaching, we see a crescendo in the Jews' objections to that teaching. When Jesus first mentions His "flesh" (v. 51), the Jews question His use of the term (v. 52). After Jesus becomes even more explicit about eating His flesh (vv. 53-58), the Jews become even more obstinate in their disbelief (v. 60). The increase in the intensity of both Jesus' language and the Jews objections correspond to each other as the scene reaches its climax.

Since Jesus has exhausted all possible methods of communicating to His disciples that they must consume His flesh and Blood (and they still don't believe Him), the only thing left for Jesus to do is remind them He is God. This is just what Jesus did at the conclusion of part one (faith) in vv. 45-47. As we stated at the outset, Jesus' disciples can believe in the Eucharist only if they believe in the Incarnation. Thus, Jesus says, "Do you take offense at this? Then what if you were to see the Son of man *ascending where he was before?*" (vv. 61-62).

Jesus describes the miracle of His future Ascension to not only reiterate His divinity, but to also castigate the Jews for their unbelief *because they have already seen His miracles.* In other words, Jesus says, "Will it take another miracle for you to believe?" The answer is No. It will not take another miracle, but the *Holy Spirit* to convict their hearts of the truth. That is why Jesus then says in v. 63: "It is the *spirit* that gives life, the flesh is of no avail; the words that I have spoken to you are spirit and life."

"The Spirit Gives Life; the Flesh Is of No Avail"

Many Protestants take v. 63 entirely out of context. It may be one of the most abused passages in Scripture. Because Jesus said, "the spirit gives life; the flesh is of no avail," the Protestant concludes that Jesus was speaking only symbolically about His flesh. In other words, after repeatedly and graphically telling His disciples to eat His flesh and drink His Blood in vv. 51-58, the

Protestants argues that Jesus now retracts His teachings in v. 63. Before, Jesus' flesh gave eternal life; now, it profited nothing. The argument is refuted not only by logic, but by Scripture itself.

Jesus used the comparison of "spirit" versus "flesh" to emphasize that one needs to be led by the Spirit of God, not the spirit of the world, to discern His teaching. Jesus does this elsewhere in Scripture.[89] If the disbelieving Jews used their natural faculties alone, they would never understand the spiritual truths of the Eucharist. The Spirit is of God; the flesh is of the world. Thus, Jesus' reference to "flesh" had nothing to do with *His* flesh, just as His use of "Spirit" had nothing to do with the *Jews'* spirit.

Paul also uses the "spirit" versus "flesh" paradigm throughout Scripture.[90] In his first letter to the Corinthians, whom Paul taught explicitly about the Eucharist, Paul emphasizes that the spiritual man discerns spiritual truths because he is led by the Spirit, while the unspiritual man is unable to understand these truths. He writes:

> Now we have received not the spirit of the world, but the Spirit which is from God, that we might understand the gifts bestowed on us by God. And we impart this in words not taught by human wisdom but taught by the Spirit, interpreting spiritual truths to those who possess the Spirit. The unspiritual man does not receive the gifts of the Spirit of God, for they are folly to him, and he is not able to understand them because they are spiritually discerned. The spiritual man judges all things, but is himself to be judged by no one.
>
> — 1 COR 2:12-15

Because the flesh prevents a man from discerning spiritual truths, it "profits nothing." Because the Spirit leads a man to

[89] See Jn 1:13; 3:6; 8:15; Mk 14:38.
[90] Rom 8:5; 1 Cor 3:3; Gal 5:17; see also Eph 2:3; 2 Pet 2:18.

understand spiritual truths, the "spirit gives life." That is because "that which is born of the Spirit is spirit" (Jn 3:6). The Jews can only understand the profound spiritual truths of the Eucharist through the Spirit, not the flesh. If they use human wisdom alone, bereft of the Spirit, they will remain unspiritual men. As we will see in the chapter on the Fathers, the entire early Church *spiritually* judged Jesus' words as *literally* referring to His flesh and blood.

We also see how Jesus first connects "life" with eating His flesh in vv. 50-51, 53-54, 57-58, and then says the Spirit gives "life" in v. 63. Because Jesus is communicating a spiritual truth, His truth not only has to be spiritually discerned, but is a *spiritual reality*. That is, Jesus is not giving us natural flesh to eat, but the supernatural flesh of the Son of God. The Jews mistook Jesus' flesh for ordinary human flesh, and that is because they mistook Jesus for an ordinary human being. Again, if we don't believe in the Incarnation, we will not believe in the Eucharist.

We also note that throughout his Gospel, John uses a literary device called *double entendre*. This is a technique that attributes different meanings to a single word or statement, and often in the same setting. John often presents Jesus' words with this objective in mind. In the very beginning of his Gospel, John refers to humans who were "born of the flesh" (Jn 1:13), and then says "the Word became flesh" (Jn 1:14). In Jn 6, John tells us the "bread" refers to both belief in Jesus (v. 35) and Jesus' flesh (v. 51); "flesh" refers to both the unspiritual (v. 63) and Jesus' body (vv. 51, 53-54, 56-57); and, "Spirit" refers to both God and the way one discerns spiritual truths (v. 63).

In v. 63, when Jesus says, "The words I have spoken are spirit and life," typically Protestants erroneously conclude that "spirit" means "symbolic." In other words, the Protestant twists Jesus' words to say "the words I have spoken are *symbolic* and life." Of course, Jesus does not say His words are symbolic, nor is there any place in Scripture where "spirit" means "symbolic." Moreover,

Jesus did not say "My *flesh* is spirit," which might have leaned toward a symbolic meaning; He said, "My *words* are spirit," which means His words had to be discerned *spiritually*, not symbolically. The spiritual words that give *life* are that we must consume Jesus' flesh and blood or we have *no life* in us.

"Do You Also Wish to Go Away?"

At this point in Jn 6, we have reached the climax of Jesus' Eucharistic discourse. Jesus has exhausted all the ways in which He can communicate His teaching to the unbelieving Jews. He has proven His divinity through miracles; He has taught in the most unmistakable terms; and He has answered all their objections. Now, the burden is on the disciples to make a decision. Will they stay with Jesus or abandon Him? John tells us, "After this many of his disciples drew back and no longer went about with him" (v. 66).

A few moments before, Jesus had told His disciples, "Him who comes to me I will not cast out" (v. 37) and "I should lose nothing of all that he has given me" (v. 39). Now, in Jn 6:66, Jesus lets His disciples go. Because Jesus promised never to cast away any who came to Him, He would not have allowed these disciples to leave under false pretenses. If the wayward disciples misunderstood Jesus, then Jesus who is Truth itself would have corrected them. Jesus, who came to give eternal life, would have corrected His disciples about their misunderstanding of what it takes to gain eternal life. He would have said, "Wait, come back here, you misunderstood Me. I was speaking figuratively, not literally!" Instead, Jesus let them go. Why? The reason is because Jesus' graphic teaching on the Eucharist "was a hard saying; who can listen to it?" (v. 60).

It was a hard saying, especially because Jesus, who always explained when He was using food as a metaphor, provided no such explanation this time. For example, while in Samaria, Jesus told His disciples, "I have food to eat of which you do not know" (Jn 4:32). When the disciples inquired about getting Jesus food to eat, He corrected them by saying, "My food is to do the will of him who sent me, and to accomplish his work" (Jn 4:34).

Jesus also warned His disciples to "beware of the leaven of the Pharisees and Sadducees" (Mt 16:6). When His disciples thought Jesus was referring to literal food, Jesus corrected them by explaining that the "leaven" referred to the Pharisees and Sadducees' teachings (Mt 16:12). About Jesus' difficult teachings, Mark says, "But privately to his own disciples he explained everything" (Mk 4:34). Jesus offered no further explanation about His teachings on the Eucharist because His disciples understood Him correctly.

Jesus then turns to His apostles and asks them, "Do you also wish to go away?" (v. 67). Peter, the future leader of the Church, answers: "Lord, to whom shall we go? You have the words of eternal life; and we have believed, and have come to know, that you are the Holy One of God" (vv. 68-69). Notice how Peter does not proclaim understanding of Jesus' teaching on the Eucharist. Instead, as he did in Matthew 16:16, Peter proclaims belief *in Jesus' divinity*, which is where we first began our analysis of Jn 6.

Peter recognized that Jesus went back to this fundamental teaching at the end of both the *faith* part (vv. 45-46) and the *action* part (v. 62) of His discourse. Imitating His Master, Peter does the same thing. Peter communicates that one must *first* believe in Christ's divinity *before* he can believe in the Eucharist, for the Eucharist is an extension of Christ's Incarnation. Thus, Jn 6 begins and ends by emphasizing the need to embrace the divinity of Jesus Christ.[91]

In concluding His discourse, Jesus rebukes those who don't believe in the Eucharist in a startling way. He tells His apostles, "Did I not choose you, the twelve, and one of you is a devil?' He

---

[91] When Jesus instituted the Eucharist a year later, He reminded His apostles of His divinity when He said, "Believe in God, believe also in me" (Jn 14:1).

spoke of Judas the son of Simon Iscariot, for he, one of the twelve, was to betray him."[92] Although many people had just abandoned Him, Jesus singles out Judas whom Satan would later enter.[93] By singling out Judas, Jesus ties unbelief in the Eucharist *to the devil himself.* Those who willfully reject the miracle of the Eucharist are of the devil, not the Spirit. They betray Jesus just as Judas betrayed Him.

Other Protestations

In light of the overwhelming evidence that Jesus was speaking literally in Jn 6, one of the more popular rebuttals is the reference to Jn 2:19, where Jesus says, "Destroy this temple, and in three days I will raise it up." In this instance, the Jews thought Jesus was speaking about the Temple in Jerusalem, but He was really speaking "of the temple of his body" (Jn 2:21). The Jews understood Jesus literally but were wrong. Thus, many Protestants conclude, the Jews understood Jesus literally in Jn 6 but were wrong as well.

This argument does not help the Protestant for a number of reasons. First, the New Testament provides no precedent that Jesus would actually destroy and rebuild the Temple in Jerusalem. Thus, the Jews did not have any precedent for their erroneous understanding. There is, however, plenty of Scriptural precedent that Jesus was going to give His Body and Blood to be consumed, as we see in the Last Supper accounts and Paul's teachings. Moreover, Jesus *did* speak about His Resurrection elsewhere in Scripture.[94] Similarly, when Protestants quote Jesus' statement, "I am the door" (Jn 10:7, 9) to show He wasn't speaking literally in Jn 6 (because Jesus is not literally a "door"), we point out that there is no biblical precedent for concluding Jesus is a door. Jn 10

---

[92] Jn 6:70-71; see also Jn 6:64.
[93] Jn 13:2, 27.
[94] Mt 16:21; 17:9, 23; 20:19; 26:32; Mk 14:28; Lk 9:22; Jn 2:19, 22.

is the only time Jesus makes such a statement, and the context is obviously metaphorical.[95] This is why no one objected, "How can this man be a door?" like they did in Jn 6 ("How can this man give us His flesh to eat?").

Second, in both Jn 2:19 and Jn 6, Jesus uses symbolic words (temple and bread) to refer to His *actual* body. Thus, the literary device Jesus uses in Jn 2:19 *parallels*, not contradicts, Jn 6. This means that the *symbol* can also represent the *reality*. For example, when Jesus says, "No sign shall be given to it except the sign of the prophet Jonah" (Mt 12:39), He was speaking of the reality of His Resurrection(sign and reality). If the sign or symbol can be the actual reality, then the bread of Jn 6 can be Jesus' actual flesh.

Third, in the same Gospel of John, Jesus uses words that appear to have one meaning, but actually point to a different and more profound meaning. For example, in Jn 3:5, Jesus says "unless one is born of water and the Spirit, he cannot enter the kingdom of God." Being reborn of water superficially suggests going back into one's mother's womb, as Nicodemus first believed (Jn 3:4). But, while "water" and "rebirth" are literal, they point to the deeper, sacramental meaning of baptism (see Jn 1:31-33). Similarly, while the use of "bread" in the Eucharist is literal, it points to the deeper meaning that we receive the sacramental flesh and blood of Jesus Christ in the Eucharist.

To maintain their position on Jn 6, Protestants are ultimately forced to conclude that Jesus deliberately misled all of His disciples. Since everyone understood Jesus literally, and Jesus knew this but didn't correct them, the Protestant concludes that the Savior deceived us. Knowing that the early Church would take

---

[95] In Jn 10:1-7, Jesus uses the words "sheepfold," "door," "thief," "robber," and "sheep" as metaphors for His teaching on following Him alone to obtain eternal life. Jesus uses a similar approach in Jn 15:1-8, when He uses "vinedresser," "vine," "branches," and "fruit."

His words literally, and countless Christians would be martyred for their belief, the Word of God who is truth itself engaged in one of the biggest deceptions in history. Although He promised the gates of hell would not prevail against the Church (Mt 16:18), Jesus allowed the Church to fall immediately into apostasy since, as we will see in the chapter on the Fathers, her entire life was centered on Christ in the Eucharist. Of course, such a conclusion is not only ludicrous but heretical, and is a major reason why Protestants become Catholics.

PHILOSOPHICAL OBJECTIONS TO THE EUCHARIST

Any honest non-Catholic should admit that the Bible gives us evidence — *significant* evidence — for the Catholic understanding of the Eucharist. Because of the undeniable evidence supporting the Catholic view, Protestants will resort to one final argument: the Catholic view is contrary to reason. They simply cannot believe that God, through His priest, would change bread and wine into Christ's Body and Blood. To the Protestant, such a process defies the laws of science and nature, and must therefore be rejected as unreasonable. Notice that the Protestant never says God *cannot* do such a thing, only that God *would not* do it. What say Catholics in response?

First, appealing to *reason* to prove a matter of *faith* is part and parcel of Protestant Christianity in general. Before the Protestant revolt in the sixteenth century, Christian truth was always determined by asking whether a doctrine was supported by the plain meaning of Scripture and the constant Tradition of the Catholic Church. The Protestant rebels abandoned these age-old criteria in favor of their own private judgment to determine truth and error. This egocentric approach to understanding God's revealed truth has resulted in the religious relativism and indifferentism we see afflicting Christianity today. The nearly 2,000-year-old Catholic

Church is now surrounded by at least 30,000 different Protestant denominations which are like wounds afflicting the Body of Christ.

Now, for the Catholic rejoinder: The mystery of the Eucharist is not contrary to reason; it is *above* reason. That is because it is a miracle, and the Catholic understanding of the miracle is backed by the very words of Jesus Christ and twenty centuries of Christian tradition. Like the doctrines of the Trinity and the Incarnation, the Eucharist is a doctrine that transcends our limited human capacity to fully understand. Nevertheless, as stated in the Introduction, it is much easier to accept the Eucharist than the Incarnation. It is more difficult to believe that the incomprehensible God would become man and submit to deicide. If we believe that God took on human flesh, then it's *less* of a leap of faith to also believe He would give us that flesh to eat under the appearance of bread and wine.

The Church uses the term *transubstantiation* to explain the process by which God changes the bread and wine into Christ's Body and Blood. The term incorporates the Aristotelian concepts of "substance" and "accidents" later used by Thomas Aquinas. *Accidents* describe what we perceive in the matter by our senses (color, texture, taste, size, smell). *Substance* describes what the matter truly is (the essence). When the priest offers Jesus' memorial sacrifice by repeating His words, "This is my body; this is my blood," transubstantiation occurs. When the priest utters these solemn words, he *consecrates* the bread and wine. The bread and wine become the substance of Jesus' Body and His Blood, even though the accidents of the bread and wine remain.[96]

---

[96] Some Christian groups, such as Lutherans, believe that the substance of the bread and wine remains along with Christ's Body and Blood. This view is incompatible with Christ's words ("This is my body"; not, for example, "Here is my body"). This view is also illogical because what is changed into another thing no longer remains after such change.

None of us would dare say God does not have the power to effect transubstantiation. Certainly, God has the power to both annihilate and create either accidents or substances, since He is the author of both of them.[97] Further, God can delegate this power to His creatures. I mentioned my debate with a Protestant about Confession. In the debate, I pointed out that my opponent and the governor were both human beings, but only one had the power to pardon criminals. The difference was that the State gave the pardoning power to the governor and not my opponent.

So it is with the Eucharist. God gives His priests the supernatural power to transubstantiate bread and wine through the words of consecration. The priest does not possess the power on his own. Instead, *God is the power behind the words.* When Peter raised up the crippled man, he said, "In the name of Jesus Christ of Nazareth, walk" (Acts 3:6). When a person is behind the words, a book is written, a debate is won, and a criminal is pardoned. When God is behind the words, a blind man sees, a crippled man walks, and a priest changes bread and wine into the Body and Blood of Jesus Christ.

We see examples of transubstantiation in Scripture. When Jesus changed water into wine at the wedding feast in Cana, this was a type of transubstantiation (Jn 2:1-11). When Jesus transformed the five loaves and two fish into enough food to feed thousands of people, this was also a kind of transubstantiation (Jn 6:1-14). Changes that take place with water are also types of transubstantiation. For example, when the temperature of water reaches $32°$ F, the accidents of the water change (from liquid to solid), but the substance stays the same (it's still H_2O). When the temperature of water reaches $212°$ F, the accidents of the water change (from liquid to gas), but the substance stays the same (it's still H_2O).

---

[97] Note that the Church does not teach that the substance of the bread and wine is annihilated but, rather, that it is changed into the Body and Blood of Christ. Annihilation of the substance would exclude a change of the substance.

In a similar but opposite way, in Holy Mass the substance of the bread and wine change (into Christ's Body and Blood), but the accidents remain the same (they still appear to be bread and wine).[98] The reality of a thing lies in its substance, not its accidents. Substance is what is beneath the surface. Water, steam, and ice still remain the substance of water, even though the accidents have changed. The substance of wine changes into the substance of Christ's blood, even though the accidents remain the same. As both Scripture and daily life show us, since God is the creator of accidents and substance, He can do with them what He pleases.

The process of metabolizing or digesting may give the best example of transubstantiation. When we consume bread and wine, the laws of nature change the bread and wine into our own flesh and blood. This natural process of our metabolism brings about the same type of change that we see in transubstantiation. If God can change bread and wine into flesh and blood through the natural law which He created, why can't He change bread and wine into flesh and blood immediately by His own power?

I have a friend who is a biomedical engineer. He talks about the mystery of the subatomic world. He explains that scientists can change one element into another by altering the nuclear structure of the atomic cell. So, while some Protestants appeal to science in their objections to transubstantiation, science itself provides no obstacles to it. If human beings can change the

---

[98] God in His Divine Providence allows the accidents to remain for two primary reasons: First, because it would be difficult, if not repugnant, to consume human flesh and blood. Instead, Christ is given to us under elements which we commonly consume, namely, bread and wine. Second, so that celebrating the Eucharist would redound to the merit of faith, which is the portal to the New Covenant. Just as in heaven we will enjoy the Vision of God through our intellects, God wills us to behold Him on earth through our intellects as well, by having faith in the Eucharist.

substance of elements through the advances of modern science (by the laws God created), then Almighty God can change the substance of elements that He created in the first place. Again, the mystery of the Eucharist is not contrary to reason; it is above it. The terms "substance" and "accidents" help us understand the Church's teaching on how the Eucharist gives us grace. When God gives us grace, He actually infuses it into our souls. Infusion is the process by which one "substance" comes into another "substance" and changes the latter. When a person consumes Jesus Christ in the Eucharist, the substance of His holy and divine nature renovates the substance of our wounded human nature. God infuses our souls with the very life of Jesus Christ who became "flesh" and is "full of grace and truth" (Jn 1:14). Thus, by receiving the Eucharist, we receive an increase of grace on earth and merit greater glory in heaven. Without this holiness, Scripture says that we will never see God (Heb 12:14).

Opponents of transubstantiation object to the Church's teaching that Jesus Christ is substantially present — Body, Blood, Soul, and Divinity — in just one drop or particle of the consecrated elements. This should not trouble the Protestant any more than the fact that the infinite God resides in our human bodies. Paul says that "the Spirit of God dwells in you" (Rom 8:9). Paul also says, "Christ is in you" (Rom 8:10). If God can dwell in our finite bodies, then Christ can be present in the Eucharist. Scripture also shows us that the risen Jesus is not subject to the laws of space or time. This is how Jesus could come to His apostles after His Resurrectioneven though the "doors were shut."[99] This is also how "every eye will see him" when He returns in glory (Apoc 1:7).

Christ's presence in the Eucharist is not much different than the soul's presence in the human body. The soul is not confined

---

[99] Jn 20:19, 26.

to any particular part of the body but is present throughout the entire body. Similarly, Christ is present in every particle or drop of the Eucharist.[100] This is why we don't refer to Christ's head, or arms, or legs in the Eucharist; those are accidents. We refer to the substance of Christ in the Eucharist, received under sacramental signs. We cannot see our souls in our bodies, but they are there. We cannot see God's Spirit dwelling within us, but He is there. And we cannot see Jesus in the Eucharist, but He is there. As Paul says, "faith is the assurance of things hoped for, the conviction of things not seen" (Heb 11:1) and "we walk by faith, not by sight" (2 Cor 5:7). Jesus also says, "Blessed are those who have not seen and yet believe" (Jn 20:29).

Anti-Catholics often make crass comments about the Eucharist. They say if Christ is really present in the consumed bread and wine, then He must come out as human waste in the digestion process. This is another example of how the Catholic Church's critics usually don't know what the Church actually teaches. The only thing "wasteful" is the ignorance of those who level such criticisms at Catholics.

First, not every thing we consume is converted by the body into a waste product. The nominal amount of consecrated bread and wine received in Holy Communion would be absorbed into the human body, not released as waste.

Second, the Church teaches that Christ remains present in the consecrated elements so long as they appear to be bread and wine (that is, the substance of Christ exists so long as the accidents of bread and wine exist). If the consecrated elements lose their appearance of bread and wine, then the presence of Christ ceases to exist. Just as God can enter a person (Rom 8:11), He can

---

[100] This is why Catholics receive Jesus under the appearance of *either* bread *or* wine. One does not have to receive Jesus under both species to receive Him completely. This is why Paul says "Whoever, therefore, eats the bread *or* drinks the cup of the Lord . . ." (1 Cor 11:27).

also leave a person (1 Sam 16:14). Once the elements cease to look like bread and wine through digestion, there is no more Real Presence. A miracle? Yes. Contrary to reason? Absolutely not.

Closing Comments

Our non-Catholic friends often tell us to have a personal relationship with Jesus. This is indeed a good thing, but how can we have a more personal relationship with Jesus than consuming His Body and Blood? Like a husband and wife who renew their covenant in the life-giving one-flesh union of marriage, Catholics renew their relationship with Christ in the Eucharist. The married couple's *personal* relationship is reinforced and enhanced in the *one-flesh* relationship. It is the same for the Catholic's relationship with Jesus Christ.

Since Christ has been raised to heaven, we come to know and love Him on earth "in the breaking of the bread." Luke reveals this to us in the Emmaus Road story, when after His Resurrection, Jesus explains the Scriptures to the two disciples and then, celebrates the Eucharist (which, incidentally, is the order of the Holy Mass to the present day). The disciples did not recognize Jesus until "he took the bread and blessed, and broke it, and gave it to them. And their eyes were opened and they recognized him; and he vanished out of their sight" (Lk 24:30-31).

Although Jesus is "out of our sight" in the Eucharist, He is present to us in the most intimate of ways, for we receive His Body, Blood, Soul, and Divinity in "the hidden manna" (Apoc 2:17). Jesus promised to be with us *always*, and He fulfills that promise in the Eucharist (Mt 28:20). In the Our Father, Jesus taught us to ask for our "daily bread."[101] Since man "does not live

---

[101] Mt 6:11; Lk 11:3. The phrase "daily bread" comes between the phrases "thy kingdom come on earth as in heaven" and "forgive us our trespasses," and thus points to the Eucharist. The Eucharist brings about the heavenly kingdom on earth and forgives our sins.

by bread alone,"[102] this daily bread refers to our spiritual sustenance, not just our natural sustenance. Both come from God, and we need both to live, physically and spiritually.

Jesus instituted the Eucharist to inaugurate the New Covenant, but the New Covenant will not be consummated until the "last day." On that day, the body of Christ (the Church) will be presented to Christ as a Bride adorned for her Husband (Apoc 21:2). Then, all the faithful will be invited to "the marriage supper of the lamb,"[103] where we will "eat and drink" in the heavenly kingdom (Lk 22:30). There, Jesus "will gird himself and have them sit at table, and he will come and serve them" (Lk 12:37). Thus, the Eucharist is a foretaste of the heavenly banquet. Adam's sin deprived us from eating of the "tree of life."[104] Now, through the sacrifice of the Second Adam, Jesus Christ, we may partake of the "tree of life" as God originally intended.[105]

As we have said from the very beginning, the Eucharist, like the Incarnation, is a profound mystery. But no other doctrine in Christianity has as much Scriptural, historical, and patristic support as the Eucharist. Jesus tells us that we must become like children to enter the kingdom of God (Mt 18:2-5). We must have childlike faith in the Eucharist, for faith is the gateway to the New Covenant. We reiterate Paul's wisdom that "the foolishness of God is wiser than men, and the weakness of God is stronger than men" (1 Cor 1:25). As the angel Gabriel told the Blessed Mother at the Incarnation of Christ: "For with God nothing will be impossible" (Lk 1:37).

No other doctrine reveals God's infinite love for us like the doctrine of the Eucharist. God took on flesh to be sacrificed for our sins and consumed for our salvation. God loves us so much

---

[102] See Mt 4:4; Deut 8:3.
[103] Apoc 19:9.
[104] See Gen 3:22-24.
[105] Apoc 2:7; 22:14.

that He wants to not only forgive us through sacrifice, but divinize us through Holy Communion. He wants us to "become partakers of the divine nature" (2 Pet 1:4). This intimate, personal, nuptial communion is the meaning of covenant *par excellence*, and it is brought about by the Holy Eucharist — the sign and seal of our New Covenant with God.

CHAPTER IV

The Early Church Fathers on the Eucharist

THE IMPORTANCE OF THE FATHERS

Up to this point, we have used Scripture alone to explain and defend the Catholic Church's teachings on the Eucharist. However, Christianity is not a "religion of the book." It is a religion of the "Word of God." Christ has given us His Word through both the Scriptures and the Apostolic Tradition, and not the Scriptures alone. Paul commands us to "stand firm and hold to the traditions which you were taught by us, either by word of mouth or by letter" (2 Thess 2:15). This Tradition, which is both oral and written, has been preserved in the Church that Christ founded upon the rock of Peter and his successors (Mt 16:18-19). This is the Holy Catholic Church, "the pillar and bulwark of the truth" (1 Tim 3:15).

The oral Tradition of the apostles is reflected in the writings of the early Church Fathers. The Fathers were closest to the apostles and the original transmission of the gospel. They received the oral apostolic Tradition that was handed down to them. Some, we believe, like Clement and Ignatius of Antioch, even received their instruction directly from the apostles themselves.[1]

---

[1] Paul mentions Clement in his letter to the Philippians (4:3). Clement was the third successor to the chair of Peter (A.D. 88–97). He is noted for his famous letter to the Corinthian church, probably around A.D. 96, wherein he exhorts them to obey the Church of Rome.

According to early Christian writings, Ignatius was ordained the bishop of Antioch by the Apostle Peter. He was also the auditor of the Apostle John. As we will see, in A.D. 107, Ignatius refers to the "Eucharist" as the "Flesh of Our Savior Jesus Christ." Ignatius may have also been the first to call the Church "Catholic" in writing in his *Letter to the Smyrnaeans*, in connection with the "Eucharist":

> The only true Eucharist is the one performed by the bishop or by him whom the bishop has appointed. Wherever the bishop is, there must be the congregation, just as wherever Jesus Christ is, there is the Catholic Church.

The writings of the Fathers reveal what the early Church believed about the Christian faith.

Fact: the early Church Fathers were *unanimous* in their Catholic understanding of the Eucharist. Not one Father disagreed. They all believed in the sacrifice of the Mass and the Real Presence. This should startle any Christian who believes otherwise. The unanimity of the Fathers on such a profound mystery demonstrates that the doctrine of the Eucharist is part of the sacred deposit of Faith. Nothing so controversial could have been held in such consensus unless it came directly from God. Indeed, the Eucharist has been revealed by God through Jesus Christ, which Jesus delivered to His apostles, and they to their successors.

Of course, the Fathers believed in the Catholic Church's understanding of the Eucharist because they were Catholics themselves. There was no other "church" around. These are the same Fathers who helped define the dogmas of the Trinity, the Incarnation, and the Hypostatic Union at the first Catholic councils — doctrines which Protestants also believe. That there is much *less* Scriptural, historical, and patristic support for these other doctrines demonstrates that the Protestant opposition to the doctrine of the Eucharist — developed by the same Fathers — is purely arbitrary.

Protestants often claim that they have "the Spirit of God" when they interpret the Scriptures. This is how they rationalize a symbolic interpretation of, say, Jn 6 and 1 Cor 10 and 11. But what about the early Christians? Didn't they have the "Spirit of God" as well? Most Protestants are not arrogant enough to claim that the early Christians, especially those taught by the apostles or their closest successors, did not have the "Spirit of God." Thus, they can respond to Catholics by saying only that "*some* of the Fathers had the Spirit, but not *all* of them." The problem with this argument is that *all* of the early Church Fathers believed in the sacrifice of the Mass and the Real Presence of Christ in the Eucharist! It is an all-or-nothing proposition.

Either the entire early Church was correct in its understanding of the Eucharist, or the Church fell immediately into apostasy after Christ's Ascension into heaven. It is one or the other. If the Church fell immediately into apostasy, then Christ did not keep His promise that "the gates of hell shall not prevail against it" (Mt 16:18). If so, untold numbers of Christians, all foreseen by Jesus Christ, have been martyred in vain over the past twenty centuries, and Christianity is the biggest religious deception in history (which commenced with the plain words of Her Founder). However, if Christ did keep His promise, then the Eucharist is the greatest gift that God has given us this side of heaven, because it is the gift of Jesus Christ Himself. Again, Christians cannot be "on the fence" when it comes to the Eucharist. Christianity, the New Covenant between God and man, lives or dies with the Eucharist.

Some Protestants point out that the Catholic Church did not use the term *transubstantiation* until the Fourth Lateran Council in 1215, as if the Catholic Church did not believe in the doctrine before Lateran IV! The reason why the Church did not formalize its doctrinal terminology until 1215 is because *the doctrine was well settled.* As we will see, the Fathers already used terms like "consecrate," "convert," "transform," "transmute," "transfigure," and "transelement" to describe the change of the bread and wine into Christ's Body and Blood. Lateran IV simply settled the terminology in an official decree by calling the change *transubstantiation.*

The Catholic Church does not dogmatize its teachings in official decrees issued by a council unless there is a reason to do so. The reason is generally either to settle a debate about a doctrine (e.g., on what terminology to use, like *transubstantiation*) or condemn a heresy. The Church defined the doctrines of the Trinity and Christology earlier in her history than the Eucharist because of the intense debates about Christ's divinity, wills, and natures. She knew that these were doctrines from which the rest of the Church's dogmas flow. As we have pointed out in this book, one must believe in the Incarnation to believe in the Eucharist.

When the Church defined the term *transubstantiation* at Lateran IV, the decree was meant to settle the ongoing debate about the terminology to be used, not to foist some novel teaching upon the Church. Similarly, when the Protestant revolutionaries attacked the Church's teaching on the Eucharist in the sixteenth century, the Council of Trent issued some of the most important decrees on the Eucharist to dispel the Protestant heresies and affirm what the Church always believed (see Appendix B). This is the same Catholic Church that condemned the heresies of such men as Arius, Macedonius, Nestorius, Pelagius, Eutyches, Albigenses, and Waldenses (first through twelfth centuries). If Protestants embrace these dogmatic pronouncements (which they do), then we must ask why they do not embrace the same Church's pronouncements on the Holy Eucharist. Seemingly it can be due only to ignorance, prejudice, or disobedience.

While the Church convoked councils to condemn the errors of heretics, *it never condemned as heretics those who held the Catholic belief in the Eucharist.* In fact, no accusation of heresy was ever uttered against any of them. Why is that? Because their belief in the Eucharist was the teaching of Jesus Christ himself. Jesus transmitted His teaching on the Eucharist through the plain words of Scripture and the Tradition of the apostles. To His apostles, Jesus said, "He who hears you hears me, and he who rejects you rejects me" (Lk 10:16). If a Protestant Christian claims he will follow only "historical" Christian teaching, then the Eucharist will be *one of the first doctrines he embraces.*

The Eucharist is the unfathomable sign of covenant unity between Christ and His true Church. It is the main reason why Protestants, Jews, and others become Catholics. The celebration of the Eucharist was the heart and soul of early Christian life since the very beginning and was not seriously questioned until the sixteenth century. The sacrifice, Real Presence, and Communion of Christ are the most historical, patristic, and biblically provable doctrines in Christianity. Let us now take a brief look at some of the writings of the early Christians on the Eucharist. Following are well-known quotes from the Fathers primarily from the first five centuries of the Church, without further commentary.

THE SACRIFICE OF THE EUCHARIST

He commanded us to celebrate sacrifices and services, and that it should not be thoughtlessly or disorderly, but at fixed times and hours. He has Himself fixed by His supreme will the places and persons whom He desires for these celebrations, in order that all things may be done piously according to His good pleasure, and be acceptable to His will. So then those who offer their oblations at the appointed seasons are acceptable and blessed, but they follow the laws of the

Master and do not sin. For to the high priest his proper ministrations, are allotted, and to the priests the proper place has been appointed, and on Levites their proper services have been imposed. The layman is bound by the ordinances for the laity . . . Our sin will not be small if we eject from the episcopate those who blamelessly and holily have offered its sacrifices.

— Clement of Rome, A.D. 88–97,
Letter to the Corinthians, Patrologiae Cursus Completus:
Series graeca, Abbe J. P. Migne (*PG*) 1, 40, 1;
after ellipsis 1, 44, 4; *Faith of the Early Fathers,*
ed. William Jurgens (*FEF*), v. 1, 19

. . . this Thy holy and spiritual table, upon which Thy only-begotten Son, and our Lord Jesus Christ, is mystically set forth as a sacrifice for me, a sinner, and stained with every spot.

— *The Divine Liturgy of James, Apostle and Brother of the*
Lord, c. A.D. 100, *Early Liturgies,* I, *The Priest,* I;
Ante Nicene, Nicene and Post Nicene Fathers, 1896, 1994
ed., Philip Schaff (*NPNF*), v. 7, p. 537.

. . . receive us as we draw near to Thy holy altar, according to the greatness of Thy mercy, that we may become worthy of offering to Thee gifts and sacrifices for our transgressions and for those of the people; and grant to us, O Lord, with all fear and a pure conscience to offer to Thee this spiritual and bloodless sacrifice, and graciously receiving it unto Thy holy and spiritual altar above the skies for an odour of a sweet spiritual smell, send down in answer on us the grace of Thy all-holy Spirit . . . and grant that our offering may be acceptable, sanctified by the Holy Spirit, as a propitiation for our transgressions and the errors of the people; and for the rest of the souls that have fallen asleep aforetime . . .

— Ibid., *NPNF*, v. 7, p. 543

And may Thy Holy Spirit come, O Lord, and rest upon this oblation of Thy servants which they offer, and bless and sanctify it; and may it be unto us, O Lord, for the propitiation of our offenses and the forgiveness of our sins . . . and through it cleanse me from the stains of my sin, and forgive me my offenses and sins, whether known or unknown to me.

— *The Liturgy of the Blessed Apostles,* c. A.D. 100,
Early Liturgies, XIII; XIV, *NPNF*, v. 7, p. 565

Hence God speaks by the mouth of Malachi, one of the twelve [prophets], as I said before, about the sacrifices at that time presented by you: "I have no pleasure in you, saith the Lord; and I will not accept your sacrifices at your hands: for from the rising of the sun unto the going down of the same, My name has been glorified among the Gentiles, and in every place incense is offered to My name, and a pure offering: for My name is great among the Gentiles, saith the Lord: but ye profane it." He then speaks of those Gentiles, namely us, who in every place offer sacrifices to Him, i.e., the bread of the Eucharist, and also the cup of the Eucharist, affirming both that we glorify His name, and that you profane it.

— Justin Martyr, A.D. 110–165,
Dialogue with Trypho; NPNF, v. 1, p. 215

On the Lord's own day, assemble in common to break Bread and offer thanks; but first confess your sins, so that your Sacrifice may be pure. However, no one quarreling with his brother may join your meeting until they are reconciled;

your Sacrifice must not be defiled. For here we have the saying of the Lord: "In every place and time offer me a pure Sacrifice; for I am a mighty King, says the Lord; and my name spreads terror among the nations."

— *The Didache*, A.D. 140, 14, 1-2; *FEF*, v. 1, 8

He took from among creation that which is bread, and gave thanks, saying, "This is My Body." He taught the new Sacrifice of the new covenant, of which Malachias, one of the twelve prophets, had signified beforehand . . . By these words, he makes plain that the former people will cease to make offerings to God; but that in every place Sacrifice will be offered to Him, and indeed, a pure one; for His name is glorified among the Gentiles.

— Irenaeus of Lyons, A.D. 140–202, *Against Heresies, 4, 17; FEF*, 232, *NPNF*, v. 1, p. 484

Does, then, the Eucharist cancel a service devoted to God, or bind it more to God? Will not your Station be more solemn if you have withal stood at God's altar? When the Lord's Body has been received and reserved, each point is secured, both the participation of the sacrifice and the discharge of duty.

— Tertullian, A.D. 160–220, *On Prayer*, xvi; *NPNF*, v. 3, p. 677

"And she [wisdom] has furnished her table" . . . refers to His honored and undefiled body and blood, which day by day are administered and offered sacrificially at the spiritual divine table, as a memorial of that first and ever-memorable table of the spiritual divine supper.

— Hippolytus, A.D. 160–235, *Fragment from Commentary on Proverbs; NPNF*, v. 5, p. 175

The priest who imitates that which Christ did, truly takes the place of Christ, and offers there in the Church a true and perfect Sacrifice to God the Father.

— Cyprian of Carthage, A.D. 200–258,
Cyprian to the Ephesians; NPNF, v. 5, p. 361

. . . and do not by human and novel institution depart from that which Christ our Master both prescribed and did; yet since some, either by ignorance or simplicity in sanctifying the cup of the Lord, and in ministering to the people, do not do that which Jesus Christ, our Lord and God, the founder and teacher of this sacrifice, did and taught . . .

— Cyprian of Carthage,
Epistle to Caecilius, 62, 1; *NPNF*, v. 5, p. 359

. . . And who is more a priest of the Most High God than our Lord Jesus Christ, who, when He offered sacrifice to God the Father, offered the very same which Melchisedech had offered, namely bread and wine, which is in fact His Body and Blood!

— Ibid., 62, 4; *NPNF*, v. 5, p. 359

Listen to what happened in my presence, before my very eyes. There was a baby girl, whose parents had fled and had, in their fear, rather improvidently left it in the charge of its nurse. The nurse took the helpless child to the magistrates. There, before the idol where the crowds were flocking, as it was too young to eat the flesh, they gave it some bread dipped in what was left of the wine offered by those who had already doomed themselves. Later, the mother recovered her child. But the girl could not reveal or tell the wicked thing that had been done, any more than she had been able to understand or ward it off before. Thus, when the mother brought her in with her while we were offering the Sacrifice, it was through ignorance that this mischance occurred . . . Moreover, when the Sacred Rites were completed and the deacon began ministering to those present, when its turn came to receive, it turned its little head away as if sensing the Divine Presence, it closed its mouth, held its lips tight, and refused to drink from the chalice. The deacon persisted and, in spite of its opposition, poured in some of the Consecrated Chalice. There followed choking and vomiting. The Eucharist could not remain in a body or mouth that was defiled; the Drink which had been sanctified by Our Lord's Blood returned from the polluted stomach. So great is the power of the Lord, and so great His majesty!

— Cyprian of Carthage, *The Lapsed*, 25; *FEF*, v. 1, 552a

We find that the cup which the Lord offered was mixed; and that what was wine, He called Blood. From this it is apparent that the Blood of Christ is not offered if there is no wine in the cup; nor is the sacrifice of the Lord celebrated with a legitimate consecration unless our offering and sacrifice corresponds to the passion.

— Cyprian of Carthage, *Epistle to Caecilius*, 62, 9; *NPNF*, v. 5, p. 361

Then upon the completion of the spiritual Sacrifice, the bloodless worship, over the propitiatory victim we call upon God for the common peace of the Churches, for the welfare of the world, for kings, for soldiers and allies, for the sick, for the afflicted; and in summary, we all pray and offer this Sacrifice for all who are in need.

— Cyril of Jerusalem, A.D. 315–386, *Catechetical Lectures, On the Mysteries*, 23, 5, 8; *NPNF* II, v. 7, p. 154

Then we make mention also of those who have already fallen asleep: first, the patriarchs, prophets, Apostles, and martyrs, that through their prayers and supplications God would receive our petition; next, we make mention also of the holy fathers and bishops who have already fallen asleep, and, to put it simply, of all among us who have already fallen asleep; for we believe that it will be of very great benefit of the souls of those for whom the petition is carried up, while this holy and most solemn Sacrifice is laid out.

— Ibid., 23, 5, 9; *NPNF* II, v. 7, p. 154

In the same way we, when we offer to Him our supplications for those who have fallen asleep, though they be sinners, weave no crown, but offer up Christ sacrificed for our sins, propitiating our merciful God for them as well as for ourselves.

— Ibid., 23, 5, 10; *NPNF* II, v. 7, pp. 154-155

It has come to the knowledge of the holy and great Synod that, in some districts and cities, the deacons administer the Eucharist to the presbyters, whereas neither canon nor custom permits that they who have no right to offer [sacrifice] should give the Body of Christ to them that do offer. And this also has been made known, that certain deacons now touch the Eucharist even before the bishops. Let all such practices be utterly done away, and let the deacons remain within their own bounds, knowing that they are the ministers of the bishop and the inferiors of the presbyters. Let them receive the Eucharist according to their order, after the presbyters, and let either the bishop or the presbyter administer to them.

— Council of Nicea, A.D. 325, *Canon XVIII*;
NPNF II, v. 14, p. 38

Cease not to pray and plead for me when you draw down the Word by your word, when in an unbloody manner cutting you cut the Body and Blood of the Lord, using your voice for a sword.

— Gregory of Nazianzus, A.D. 330–389, *Letter to Amphilochius*, 171; *NPNF* II, v. 7, p. 469

Even if one does not now see Christ is sacrificed, still He Himself is sacrificed on earth, whenever the body of Christ is sacrificed, Yea, it is obvious that He even offers Himself in us, for His Word sanctifies that sacrifice which is offered.

— Ambrose, A.D. 340–397, *Psalm 38, 25*; *Fundamentals of Catholic Dogma*, Ludwig Ott (*FCD*), p. 406

We follow, inasmuch as we are able, being priests; and we offer the sacrifice on behalf of the people. And even if we are of but little merit, still, in the sacrifice, we are honorable. For even if Christ is not now seen as the one who offers the sacrifice, nevertheless, it is He Himself that is offered. Indeed, to offer Himself He is made visible in us, He whose word makes holy the sacrifice that is offered.

— Ambrose, *On Twelve Psalms; Patrologiae Cursus Completus: Series latina*, Abbe J. P. Migne (*PL*), 14, 38, 25; *FEF*, v. 2, 1260

Wherefore the consecrated priest ought to be as pure as if he were standing in the heavens themselves in the midst of this power . . . For when thou seest the Lord sacrificed, and laid upon the altar, and the priest standing and praying over the victim, and all the worshipers empurpled with that precious blood, canst thou then think that thou art still amongst men and standing upon earth? Art thou not, on the contrary, straightway translated into Heaven . . . [?] He who sitteth on high with the Father is at that hour held in the hands of all.

— John Chrysostom, A.D. 344–407,
On the Priesthood,
PG 47, 3, 4, 177; *FEF,* 1118

I wish to add something that is plainly awe-inspiring, but do not be astonished or upset. This Sacrifice, no mater who offers it, be it Peter or Paul, is always the same as that which Christ gave His disciples and which priests now offer: The offering of today is in no way inferior to that which Christ offered, because it is not men who sanctify the offering of today; it is the same Christ who sanctified His own. For just as the words which God spoke are the very same as those which the priest now speaks, so too the oblation is the very same.

— John Chrysostom,
Homilies on the Second Epistle to Timothy,
II; *NPNF,* v. 13, p. 483

By this reasoning, since the sacrifice is offered everywhere, are there, then, a multiplicity of Christs? By no means! Christ is one everywhere. He is complete here, complete there, one Body. And just as He is one Body and not many though offered everywhere, so too is there one Sacrifice.

— John Chrysostom, *Homilies on the Epistle to the Hebrews; PG,* 63, 17, 3; *FEF,* 1222

Following the dismissal from the Martyrium, everyone proceeds behind the cross, where, after a hymn is sung and a prayer is said, the bishop offers the sacrifice and everyone receives Communion. Except on this day, throughout the year the sacrifice is never offered behind the cross save on this day alone.

— Egeria, A.D. 345–399,
Diary of a Pilgrimage, Ch. 35

All of the proper passages from the Book of Moses were read, the sacrifice was offered in the prescribed manner, and we received Communion.

— Ibid., Ch. 3

Holy, holy, holy Lord Sabaoth, heaven and earth is full of your glory. Heaven is full, and full is the earth with your magnificent glory, Lord of Virtues. Full also is this Sacrifice, with your strength and your communion; for to You we offer this living Sacrifice, this unbloody oblation.

— Serapion, c. A.D. 350, *The Sacramentary of Serapion,
Prayer of the Eucharistic Sacrifice*, 13

All the priests of the new covenant offer the same sacrifice continually, in every place and in every age; because the sacrifice which was offered for all is also one — the sacrifice of Christ our Lord, who accepted death for us, and by the offering of that sacrifice has purchased salvation for us, as blessed Paul says, "By one oblation," he says indeed, "He hath perfected for ever them that are sanctified" (Heb 10:14).

— Theodore of Mopsuestia, A.D. 350–428,
Catechetical Homilies, 19; *FEF*, v. 2, 1113f

Was not Christ once for all offered up in His own person as a sacrifice? . . . For if sacraments had not some points of real resemblance to the things of which they are the sacraments, they would not become sacraments at all. In most cases, moreover, they do in virtue of this likeness bear the name of the realities which they resemble. As, therefore, in a certain manner the sacrament of Christ's body is Christ's body, and the sacrament of Christ's blood is Christ's blood, in the same manner the sacrament of faith is faith.

> — Augustine, A.D. 354–430, *Letters* 98, 9;
> *FEF,* 1424; *NPNF,* v. 1, p. 410

For the whole Church observes this practice which was handed down by the Fathers; that it prays for those who have died in the communion of the Body and Blood of Christ, when they are commemorated in their own place in the Sacrifice of itself; and the Sacrifice is offered also in memory of them on their behalf.

> — Augustine, *Sermons; PL* 38, 172, 2; *FEF,* v. 1516

The fact that our fathers of old offered sacrifices with beasts for victims, which the present-day people of God read about but do not do, is to be understood in no way but this: that those things signified the things that we do in order to draw near to God and to recommend to our neighbor the same purpose. A visible Sacrifice, therefore, is the sacrament, that is to say, the sacred sign, of an invisible sacrifice.

> — Augustine, *The City of God;*
> *PL* 41, 10, 5; *NPNF,* v. 2, p. 183

Christ is both Priest, offering Himself, and Himself the Victim. He willed that the sacramental sign of this should be the daily Sacrifice of the Church, who, since the Church is His body and He the Head, learns to offer herself through Him.

> — Ibid., *PL* 41, 10, 20;
> *NPNF,* v. 2, p. 193, *FEF* 1744

By those sacrifices of the Old Law, this one Sacrifice is signified, in which there is a true remission of sins; but not only is no one forbidden to take as food the Blood of this Sacrifice, rather, all who wish to possess life are exhorted to drink thereof.

> — Augustine, *Questions on the Heptateuch*;
> *PL* 34, 3, 57; *FEF*, v. 3, 1866

Nor can it be denied that the souls of the dead find relief through the piety of their friends and relatives who are still alive, when the Sacrifice of the Mediator is offered for them, or when alms are given in the church . . .

> — Augustine, *Enchiridion of Faith, Hope and Love*;
> *PL* 40, 29, 109; *FEF*, v. 3, 1930

Open your eyes at last, then, any time and see, from the rising of the sun to its setting, the Sacrifice of Christians is offered, not in one place only, as was established with you Jews, but everywhere; and not to just any god at all, but to Him who foretold it, the God of Israel . . . Not in one place, as was prescribed for you in the earthly Jerusalem, but in every place, even in Jerusalem herself. Not according to the order of Aaron, but according to the order of Mechisedech.

> — Augustine, *Sermon Against the Jews;*
> *PL* 42, 9, 13; *FEF*, v. 3, 1977

The angels surround the priest; the whole sanctuary and the space before the altar is filled with the heavenly powers who come to honor Him Who is present upon the altar . . . Behold the royal table. The angels serve at it.

> — Augustine, *The Priesthood,* 6, 4;
> *NPNF*, v. 9, p. 76

Reverence now, oh reverence, this Table whereof we all are partakers! (1 Cor 10:16-18). Christ, Who was slain for us, the Victim is placed thereon! (Heb. 13:10).

— Augustine, *Homilies on the Book of Romans*,
8, v. 21; *NPNF*, v. 11, p. 394

And whenever he [the priest] invokes the Holy Spirit, and offers the most dread sacrifice, and constantly handles the common Lord of all, tell me what rank shall we give him?
— Augustine, *The Priesthood*, 6, 4; *NPNF*, v. 9, p. 76

In ancient times, because men were very imperfect, God did not scorn to receive the blood which they were offering to idols. He did this to draw them away from those idols . . . But now He has transferred the priestly action to what is most awesome and magnificent. He has changed the sacrifice itself, and instead of the butchering of dumb beasts, He commands the offering up of Himself.

— Augustine,
Homilies on the First Epistle to the Corinthians;
PG 61, 24, 2; *FEF*, 1193

Not in vain was it decreed by the Apostles that in the awesome Mysteries remembrance should be made of the departed. They knew that here there was much gain for them, much benefit. For when the entire people stand with hands uplifted, a priestly assembly, and that awesome sacrificial Victim is laid out, how, when we are calling upon God, should we not succeed in their defense? But this is done for those who have departed the faith.

— Augustine,
Homilies on the Epistle to the Philippians;
PG 62, 3, 4; *FEF*, 1206

For this reason do you also, now the Lord is risen, offer your sacrifice, concerning which He made a constitution by us, saying, "Do this for a remembrance of me" . . . And let this be an everlasting ordinance till the consummation of the world, until the Lord come.

— *Apostolic Constitutions*, A.D. 400, 5, 3, 19;
NPNF, v. 7, p. 447

And when He had delivered to us the representative mysteries of His precious body and blood . . . Instead of a bloody sacrifice, He has appointed that reasonable and unbloody mystical one of His body and blood . . . We also, our Father, thank Thee for the precious blood of Jesus Christ, which was shed for us, and for His precious body, whereof we celebrate this representation, as Himself appointed us, "to show forth his death."

— *Apostolic Constitutions*, 5, 14; 6, 23; 7, 25;
NPNF, v. 7, pp. 444, 461, 470

We will necessarily add this also. Proclaiming the death, according to the flesh, of the Only-begotten Son of God, that is Jesus Christ, confessing his resurrection from the dead, and his ascension into heaven, we offer the unbloody Sacrifice in the churches, and so go on to the mystical thanksgivings, and are sanctified, having received his Holy Flesh and the Precious Blood of Christ the Savior of us all.

— Council of Ephesus, A.D. 431,
Session I, Letter of Cyril to Nestorius;
NPNF II, v. 14, p. 203

We perform in the churches the holy, life-giving, and unbloody sacrifice; the body, as also the precious blood, which is exhibited we believe not to be that of a common man and of anyone like unto us, but receiving it rather as his

own body and as the blood of the Word which gives all
things life. . . . Since therefore Nestorius and those who
think with him rashly dissolve the power of this mystery;
therefore it was convenient that this anathematism should
be put forth.

> — Council of Ephesus, *Session I, Can XI,* notes;
> *NPNF* II, v. 14, p. 217

This Victim alone saves the soul from eternal ruin, the sacrificing of which presents to us in a mystical way the death
of the Only-begotten, who . . . is immolated for us again in
this mystery of sacred oblation. For His body is eaten there,
His flesh is distributed among the people unto salvation, His
blood is poured out, no longer in the hands of the faithless
but in the mouth of the faithful. Let us take thought, therefore, of what this sacrifice means for us, which is in constant
representation of the suffering of the Only-begotten Son, for
the sake of our forgiveness.

> — Pope Gregory the Great, A.D. 540–604,
> *Dialogues; PL* 65, 62; *FEF*, v. 3, 2270

For to his own church, where the pastoral administration
had been given him, he ordered that water with wine should
be used at the unbloody sacrifice, so as to show forth the
mingling of the blood and water which for the life of the
whole world and for the redemption of its sins, was poured
forth from the precious side of Christ our Redeemer . . .

> — Council of Quinisext, A.D. 692,
> *Canon XXXII; NPNF* II, v. 14, p. 38

. . . they delivered to us directions for the mystical sacrifice
in writing, declared that the holy chalice is consecrated in the
Divine Liturgy with water and wine. And the holy Fathers
who assembled at Carthage provided these express terms:

"That in the holy Mysteries nothing besides the body and blood of the Lord be offered, as the Lord himself laid down, that is bread and wine mixed with water. Therefore, if any bishop or presbyter shall not perform the holy action according to what has been handed down by the Apostles, and shall not offer the sacrifice with wine mixed with water, let him be deposed, as imperfectly showing forth the mystery and innovating on the things which have been handed down."

— Ibid.

THE REAL PRESENCE OF CHRIST IN THE EUCHARIST

Consider how contrary to the mind of God are the heterodox in regard to the grace of God which has come to us. They have no regard for charity, none for the widow, the orphan, the oppressed, none for the man in prison, the hungry or the thirsty. They abstain from the Eucharist and from prayer, because they do not admit that the Eucharist is the Flesh of our Savior Jesus Christ, the same Flesh which suffered for our sins and which the Father, in His graciousness, raised from the dead.

— Ignatius of Antioch, A.D. 107,
Letter to the Smyrnaeans, 6, 2;
FEF, v. 1, 64; *NPNF*, v. 1 ch. 7, p. 89

I have no taste for the food that perishes nor for the pleasures of this life. I want the Bread of God which is the Flesh of Christ, who was the seed of David; and for drink I desire His Blood which is love that cannot be destroyed.

— Ignatius of Antioch, *Letter to the Romans, 7*;
NPNF, v. 1, p. 77

Take care, then who belong to God and to Jesus Christ — they are with the bishop. And those who repent and come to the unity of the Church — they too shall be of God, and will be living according to Jesus Christ. Do not err, my brethren: if anyone follow a schismatic, he will not inherit the Kingdom of God. If any man walk about with strange doctrine, he cannot lie down with the passion. Take care, then, to use one Eucharist, so that whatever you do, you do according to God: for there is one Flesh of our Lord Jesus Christ, and one cup in the union of His Blood; one altar, as there is one bishop with the presbytery and my fellow servants, the deacons.

— Ignatius of Antioch,
Letter to the Philadelphians,
3:2-4:1; *NPNF*, v. 1, pp. 80-81

Come together in common, one and all without exception in charity, in one faith and in one Jesus Christ, Who is of the race of David according to the Flesh, the Son of Man, and the Son of God, so that with undivided mind you may obey the bishop and the presbyters, and break one Bread which is the medicine of immortality and the antidote against death, enabling us to live forever in Jesus Christ.

— Ignatius of Antioch,
Letter to the Ephesians,
20; *NPNF*, v. 1, p. 57

This food we call the Eucharist, of which no one is allowed to partake except one who believes that the things we teach are true, and has received The Washing for forgiveness of sins and for rebirth, and who lives as Christ handed down to us. For we do not receive these things as common bread or common drink; but as Jesus Christ our Savior being incarnate by God's Word took Flesh and Blood for our salvation, so also we have been taught that the food Consecrated by the Word of prayer which comes from Him, from which our flesh and blood are nourished by transformation, is the Flesh and Blood of that incarnate Jesus.

— Justin Martyr, A.D. 110–165,
First Apology, 66;
NPNF, v. 1, p. 185

Let no one eat and drink of your Eucharist but those Baptized in the Name of the Lord; to this, too the saying of the Lord is applicable: "Do not give to dogs what is sacred."

— *The Didache,* A.D. 140, 9, 5; *FEF*, v. 1, 6

The bread over which thanks has been given is the body of their Lord, and the cup His blood . . .

— Irenaeus of Lyons, A.D. 140–202,
Against Heresies, 4, 18, 4; *NPNF* v. 1, p. 486

But our opinion is in accordance with the Eucharist, and the Eucharist in turn establishes our opinion. For we offer to Him His own, announcing consistently the fellowship and union of the flesh and Spirit. For as the bread, which is produced from the earth, when it receives the invocation of God, is no longer common bread, but the Eucharist, consisting of two realities, earthly and heavenly; so also our bodies, when they receive the Eucharist, are no longer corruptible, having the hope of the resurrection to eternity.

— Ibid., 4, 18, 5; *NPNF* v. 1, p. 486

So then, if the mixed cup and the manufactured bread receive the Word of God and become the Eucharist, that is to say, the Blood and Body of Christ, which fortify and build up the substance of our flesh, how can these people claim that the flesh is incapable of receiving God's gift of eternal life, when it is nourished by Christ's Blood and Body and is His member?

— Ibid., 5, 2, 2-3; *NPNF,* v. 1, p. 528

The Word is everything to a child; both Father and Mother, both Instructor and Nurse. "Eat My Flesh," He says, "and drink My Blood." The Lord supplies us with these intimate nutrients. He delivers over His Flesh, and pours out His Blood; and nothing is lacking for the growth of His children. O incredible mystery!

— Clement of Alexandria, A.D. 150–216,
Homilies on the Epistle to the Philippians;
PG 62, 3, 4; *FEF,* 1206

Then, having taken the bread and given it to His disciples, He made it His own body, by saying, "This is my body," that is, the figure of my body. A figure, however, there could not have been, unless there were first a veritable body. An empty thing, or phantom, is incapable of a figure . . . And thus, casting light, as He always did, upon the ancient prophesies[sic], he declared plainly enough what He meant by the bread, when He called the bread His own body. He likewise, when mentioning the cup and making the New Testament to be sealed "in His blood," affirms the reality of His body. For no blood can belong to a body which is not a body of flesh.

— Tertullian, A.D. 160–220,
Against Marcion, IV, xl; *NPNF,* v. 3, p. 418

These two baptisms He sent out from the wound in His pierced side, in order that they who believed in His blood

might be bathed with the water; they who had been bathed in the water might likewise drink the blood.
— Tertullian, *On Baptism*, xvi; *NPNF*, v. 3, p. 677

I wish to admonish you with examples from your religion. You are accustomed to take part in the Divine Mysteries, so you know how, when you have received the Body of the Lord, you reverently exercise every care lest a particle of it fall and lest anything of the Consecrated Gift perish. You account yourselves guilty, and rightly do you so believe, if any of it be lost through negligence.
— Origen, A.D. 185–254, *Homilies in Exodus*;
PG, 13, 13, 3; *FEF*, v. 1, 490

"Unless ye eat the flesh of the Son of Man, and drink His blood, ye have no life in you . . ." — then the flesh thus spoken of is that of the Lamb that takes away the sin of the world . . . Again, we eat the flesh of the Lamb, with bitter herbs, and unleavened bread, when we repent of our sins and grieve with sorrow which is according to God . . .
— Origen, *Commentary on John*, 10, 13;
NPNF, v. 9, p. 390

Also in the same place: "'Unless ye eat the flesh of the Son of man, and drink His blood, ye shall not have life in you." That it is of small account to be baptized and to receive the Eucharist, unless one profit by it both in deeds and works.
— Cyprian of Carthage, A.D. 200–258,
The Treatises of Cyprian, xii,
Third Book, Testimonies, 25, 26

And we ask that this bread should be given to us daily, that we who are in Christ, and daily receive the Eucharist for the food of salvation, may not, by the interposition of some heinous sin, by being prevented . . . from partaking of the heavenly bread, be separated from Christ's body as He Himself predicts, and warns, "I am the bread of life which came down from heaven. If any man eat of my bread, he shall live for ever; and the bread which I will give is my flesh, for the life of the world." When, therefore, He says, that whoever shall eat of His bread shall live for ever; as it is manifest that those who partake of His body and receive the Eucharist by the right of communion are living, so, on the other hand, we must fear and pray lest anyone who, being withheld from communion, is separated from Christ's body should remain at a distance from salvation; as He Himself threatens, and says, "'Unless ye eat the flesh of the Son of man, and drink His blood, ye shall have no life in you." And therefore we ask that our bread — that is, Christ — may be given to us daily, that we who abide and live in Christ may not depart from His sanctification and body.

— Ibid., 1, 8; *NPNF*, v. 5, p. 424

But the Lord was not yet arrested. After having spoken thus, the Lord rose up from the place where He had made the Passover and had given His Body as food and His Blood as drink, and He went with His disciples to the place where He was to be arrested. But He ate of His own Body and drank of His own Blood, while He was pondering on the dead. With His own hands the Lord presented His own Body to be eaten, and before he was crucified He gave His Blood as drink; and He was taken at night on the fourteenth, and was judged until the sixth hour; and at the sixth hour they condemned Him and raised Him on the cross.

— Aphraates the Persian Sage, A.D. 280–345,
Treatises, 12, 6; *FEF*, v. 1, 689

The Savior also, since He was changing the typical for the spiritual, promised them they should no longer eat the flesh of a lamb, but His own, saying, "Take, eat and drink; this is My body, and My blood." When we are thus nourished by these things, we also, my beloved, shall truly keep the feast of the Passover.

— Athanasius, A.D. 295–373,
Easter Letter IV, 4; NPNF II, v. 4, p. 517

You shall see the Levites bringing loaves and a cup of wine, and placing them on the table. So long as the prayers of supplication and entreaties have not been made, there is only bread and wine. But after the great and wonderful prayers have been completed, then the bread has become the Body, and the wine the Blood, of our Lord Jesus Christ.

— Athanasius,
Fragment of *Sermon to the Newly Baptized*;
PG 26, 1325; *FEF*, v. 2, 802

And extending His hand, He gave them the Bread which His right hand had made holy: "Take, all of you eat of this; which My word has made holy. Do not now regard as bread that which I have given you; but take, eat this Bread, and do not scatter the crumbs; for what I have called My Body, that it is indeed. One particle from its crumbs is able to sanctify thousands and thousands, and is sufficient to afford life to those who eat of it . . . And whoever eats in belief the Bread made holy in My name, if he be pure, he will be preserved in his purity; and if he be a sinner, he will be forgiven. But if anyone despise it or reject it or treat it with ignominy, it may be taken as certainty that he treats with ignominy the Son, who called it and actually made it to be His Body."

— Ephraim Syrus, A.D. 306–373,
Homilies, 4, 4; *FEF,* v. 1, 707

After the disciples had eaten the new and holy Bread, and when they understood by faith that they had eaten of Christ's body, Christ went on to explain and to give them the whole Sacrament. He took and mixed a cup of wine. Then He blessed it, and signed it, and made it holy, declaring that it was His own Blood, which was about to be poured out . . . Christ commanded them to drink, and He explained to them that the cup which they were drinking was His own Blood: "This is truly My Blood, which is shed for all of you. Take, all of you, drink of this, because it is a new covenant in My Blood, As you have seen Me do, do you also in My memory. Whenever you are gathered together in My name in Churches everywhere, do what I have done, in memory of Me, Eat My Body, and drink My Blood, a covenant new and old."

— Ibid., *FEF,* v. 1, 708

When we speak of the reality of Christ's nature being in us, we would be speaking foolishly and impiously — had we not learned it from Him. For He Himself says: "My Flesh is truly Food, and My Blood is truly Drink. He that eats My Flesh and drinks My Blood will remain in Me and I in him." As to the reality of His Flesh and Blood, there is no room left for doubt, because now, both by the declaration of the Lord Himself and by our own faith, it is truly the Flesh and it is truly Blood. And These Elements bring it about, when taken and consumed, that we are in Christ and Christ is in us. Is this not true? Let those who deny that Jesus Christ is true God be free to find these things untrue. But

He Himself is in us through the flesh and we are in Him, while that which we are with Him is in God.

— Hilary of Poitiers, A.D. 315–367, *The Trinity*, 8, 14; *NPNF* II, v. 9, p. 141

We have been instructed in these matters and filled with an unshakable faith, that that which seems to be bread, is not bread, though it tastes like it, but the Body of Christ, and that which seems to be wine, is not wine, though it too tastes as such, but the Blood of Christ . . . draw inner strength by receiving this bread as spiritual food and your soul will rejoice.

— Cyril of Jerusalem, *Catechetical Lectures, On the Mysteries*, 22, 9; *NPNF* II, v. 7, p. 152

For he has just distinctly said, (That our Lord Jesus Christ the same night in which He was betrayed, took bread, and when He had given thanks He brake it, and said, Take, eat, this is My Body: and having taken the cup and given thanks, He said, Take, drink, this is My Blood) [1 Cor 11:23-25]. Since then He Himself has declared and said of the Bread, (This is My Body), who shall dare to doubt any longer? And since He has affirmed and said, (This is My Blood), who shall ever hesitate, saying, that it is not His blood?

— Ibid., *NPNF* II, v. 7, p. 151

He once in Cana of Galilee, turned the water into wine, akin to blood, and is it incredible that He should have turned wine into blood? When called to a bodily marriage, He miraculously wrought that wonderful work; and on the children of the bride chamber, shall He not much rather be acknowledged to have bestowed the fruition of His Body and Blood?

— Ibid., 22, 4, 2; *NPNF* II, v. 7, p. 151

Contemplate therefore the Bread and Wine not as bare elements, for they are, according to the Lord's declaration, the Body and Blood of Christ; for though sense suggests this to thee, let faith establish thee. Judge not the matter from taste, but from faith be fully assured without misgiving, that thou hast been vouchsafed the Body and Blood of Christ.

— Ibid., p. 152

Then having sanctified ourselves by these spiritual Hymns, we beseech the merciful God to send forth His Holy Spirit upon the gifts lying before Him; that He may make the Bread the Body of Christ, and the Wine the Blood of Christ; for whatsoever the Holy Ghost has touched, is surely sanctified and changed.

— Ibid., p. 154

After this you hear the singing which invites you with a divine melody to the Communion of the Holy Mysteries, and which says, "Taste and see that the Lord is good." Do not trust to the judgment of the bodily palate — no, but to unwavering faith. For they who are urged to taste do not taste of bread and wine, but to the antitype, of the Body and Blood of Christ.

— Ibid., p. 156

Then after thou hast partaken of the Body of Christ, draw near also to the Cup of His Blood; not stretching forth thine hands, but bending, and saying with an air of worship and reverence, Amen, hallow thyself by partaking also of the

Blood of Christ. And while the moisture is still on thy lips, touch it with thine hands, and hallow thine eyes and brow and the other organs of sense. Then wait for the prayer, and give thanks unto God, who hath accounted thee worthy of so great mysteries.

— Ibid.

We see that the Savior took [something] in His hands, as it is in the Gospel, when He was reclining at the supper; and He took this, and giving thanks, He said: "This is really Me." And He gave to His disciples and said: "This is really Me." And we see that It is not equal or similar, not to the incarnate image, not to the invisible divinity, not to the outline of His limbs. For It is round of shape, and devoid of feeling. As to Its power, He means to say even of Its grace, "This is really Me"; and none disbelieves His word. For anyone who does not believe the truth in what He says is deprived of grace and of a Savior.

— Epiphanius of Salamis, A.D. 315–403,
The Man Well-Anchored, 57; *FEF*, v. 2, 1084

What is the mark of a Christian? That he be purified of all defilement of the flesh and of the spirit in the Blood of Christ, perfecting sanctification in the fear of God and the love of Christ, and that he have no blemish nor spot nor any such thing; that he be holy and blameless and so eat the Body of Christ and drink His Blood; for "he that eateth and drinketh unworthily, eateth and drinketh judgment to himself." What is the mark of those who eat the Bread and drink the Cup of Christ? That they keep in perpetual remembrance Him who died for us and rose again.

— Basil the Great, A.D. 329–379,
The Morals, 22

To communicate each day and to partake of the holy Body and Blood of Christ is good and beneficial; for He says quite plainly: "He that eats My Flesh and drinks My Blood has eternal life." Who can doubt that to share continually in life is the same thing as having life abundantly? We ourselves communicate four times each week, on Sunday, Wednesday, Friday and Saturday; and on other days if there is a commemoration of any saint.

— Basil the Great,
Letter to a Patrician Lady, 93

Rightly then, do we believe that the bread consecrated by the word of God has been made over into the Body of the God the Word. For that Body was, as to its potency bread; but it has been consecrated by the lodging there of the Word, who pitched His tent in the flesh.

— Gregory of Nyssa, A.D. 335–394,
The Great Catechism, 37:9-13;
NPNF II, v. 5, p. 505

He offered Himself for us, Victim and Sacrifice, and Priest as well, and "Lamb of God who takes away the sin of the world." When did He do this? When He made His own Body food and His own Blood drink for His disciples; for this much is clear enough to anyone, that a sheep cannot be eaten by a man unless its being eaten be preceded by its being slaughtered. This giving of His own Body to His disciples for eating clearly indicates that the Sacrifice of the Lamb has now been completed.

— Gregory of Nyssa,
Orations and Sermons, Jaeger, vol. 9, p. 287

The bread is at first common bread; but when the mystery sanctifies it, it is called and actually becomes the Body of Christ.

— Ibid., pp. 225-226

Now we, as often as we receive the sacramental elements, which by the mysterious efficacy of holy prayer are transformed into the Flesh and Blood, "do until the Lord's Death."

— Ambrose, A.D. 340–397,
On the Christian Faith, 4, 125; *NPNF* II, v. 10, p. 278

And so, by footstool is understood earth, but by the earth the Flesh of Christ, which we this day also adore in the mysteries, and which the apostles, as we said above, adored in the Lord Jesus.

— Ambrose, *On the Holy Spirit*, III,
79, *NPNF* II, v. 10, p. 147

You perhaps say: "My bread is usual." But the bread is bread before the words of the sacrament. When consecration has been added, from bread it becomes the flesh of Christ. So let us confirm this, how it is possible that what is bread is the body of Christ. By what words, then, is the consecration and by whose expressions? By those of the Lord Jesus. For all the rest that are said in the preceding are said by the priest: praise to God, prayer is offered, there is a petition for the people, for kings, for the rest. When it comes to performing a venerable sacrament, then the priest uses not his own expressions, but he uses the expressions of Christ. Thus, the expression of Christ performs this sacrament.

— Ambrose, *The Sacraments*,
PL, 16, 4, 4, 14; *FEF*, v. 2, 1339

Perhaps you will say, "I see something else, how is it that you assert that I receive the Body of Christ?" . . . Let us prove that this is not what nature made, but what the blessing consecrated, and the power of blessing is greater than that of nature, because by blessing, nature itself has changed . . . For that sacrament which you receive is made what it is by the word of Christ. But if the word of Elijah had such power as to bring down fire from heaven, shall not the word of Christ have power to change the nature of the elements?

> — Ambrose, *On the Mysteries*, 9, 50-52,
> *NPNF* II, v. 10, p. 324

It is the true Flesh of Christ which was crucified and buried, this is then truly the Sacrament of His Body. The Lord Jesus Himself proclaims: "This is My Body." Before the blessing of the heavenly words another nature is spoken of, after the consecration the Body is signified. He Himself speaks of His Blood. Before the consecration it has another name, after it is called Blood. Christ, then, feeds His Church with these sacraments, by means of which the substance of the soul is strengthened.

> — Ibid.

He hath given to those who desire Him not only to see Him, but even to touch, and eat Him, and fix their teeth into His flesh, and to embrace Him, and satisfy all their love.

> — John Chrysostom, *Homilies on John,* 46, 3;
> *NPNF*, v. 14, p. 166

It is not the power of man which makes what is put before us the Body and Blood of Christ, but the power of Christ Himself who was crucified for us. The priest standing there in the place of Christ says these words but their power and grace are from God. "This is My Body," he says, and these words transform what lies before him.

— John Chrysostom,
Homilies on the Treachery of Judas,
1, 6; *FEF*, v. 2, 1157

. . . therefore, lest they should be troubled then likewise, He first did this Himself, leading them to the calm participation of the mysteries. Therefore He Himself drank His own blood.

— John Chrysostom,
Homilies on Matthew, 82, 1;
NPNF, v. 10, p. 492

For neither was it enough for Him to be made man, to be smitten and slaughtered, but He also commingleth Himself with us, and not by faith only, but also in very deed maketh us His body . . . but He Himself feeds us with His own blood, and by all means entwines us with Himself. . . .With each one of the faithful doth He mingle Himself in the mysteries, and whom He begat, He nourishes by Himself, and putteth not out to another.

— Ibid., 82, 5; *NPNF*, v. 10, p. 495

The cup of blessing which we bless, is it not communion of the Blood of Christ? Very trustworthily and awesomely does he say it. For what he is saying is this: What is in the cup is that which flowed from His side, and we partake of it. He called it a cup of blessing because when we hold it in our hands that is how we praise Him in song, wondering and astonished at His indescribable Gift, blessing Him because of His having poured out this very Gift so that we might not remain in error, and not only for His having poured It out, but also for His sharing It with all of us.

> — John Chrysostom,
> *Homilies on the First Letter to the Corinthians*;
> *PG* 61, 24, I; *NPNF*, v. 12, p. 139

After the type had been fulfilled by the Passover celebration and He had eaten the flesh of the lamb with His Apostles, He takes bread which strengthens the heart of man, and goes on to the true Sacrament of the Passover, so that just as Melchizedek, the priest of the Most High God, in prefiguring Him, made bread and wine an offering, He too makes Himself manifest in the reality of His own Body and Blood.

> — Jerome, A.D. 347–419,
> *Commentaries on the Gospel of Matthew*, 4, 26, 26;
> *FEF*, v. 2, 1390

When [Christ] gave the bread he did not say, "This is the symbol of my body," but, "This is my body." In the same way, when he gave the cup of his blood he did not say, "This is the symbol of my blood," but, "This is my blood," for he wanted us to look upon them after their reception of grace and the coming of the Holy Spirit not according to their nature, but receive them as they are, the body and blood of our Lord. We ought . . . not regard them merely as bread and cup, but as the body and blood of the Lord, into which they were transformed by the descent of the Holy Spirit.

> — Theodore of Mopsuestia, A.D. 350–428,
> *Catechetical Homilies*, 5:1; *FEF*, v. 2, 1113ff

For He received earth from earth; because flesh is from the earth, and He took flesh from the flesh of Mary. He walked here in the same flesh, and gave us the same flesh to be eaten unto salvation. But no one eats that flesh unless first he adores it; and thus it is discovered how such a footstool of the Lord's feet is adored; and not only do we not sin by adoring, we do sin by not adoring.

— Augustine, *On the Psalms*, 98, 9;
NPNF, v. 8, p. 485; *FEF,* 1479a

For I promised you, who have now been baptized, a sermon in which I would explain the Sacrament of the Lord's Table, which you now look upon and of which you last night were made participants. You ought to know what you have received, what you are going to receive, and what you ought to receive daily. That Bread which you see on the altar, having been sanctified by the word of God, is the Body of Christ. The chalice, or rather, what is in that chalice, having been sanctified by the word of God, is the Blood of Christ.

— Augustine, *Sermons,* 227, 21; *FEF,* v. 3, 1519

And he was carried in his own hands. But, brethren, how is it possible for a man to do this? Who can understand it? Who is it that is carried in his own hands? A man can be carried in the hands of another; but no one can be carried in his own hands. How this should be understood literally of David, we cannot discover; but we can discover how it is meant of Christ. For Christ was carried in his own hands, when, referring to His own Body, He said, "This is My Body." For He carried that Body in His hands.

— Augustine, *On the Psalms,* 33, 1, 10;
FEF, 1464; *NPNF,* v. 8. p. 73

Christ said indicating (the bread and wine): "This is My Body," and "This is My Blood," in order that you might not judge what you see to be a mere figure. The offerings, by the hidden power of God Almighty, are changed into Christ's Body and Blood, and by receiving these we come to share in the life-giving and sanctifying efficacy of Christ.

— Cyril of Alexandria, A.D. 376–444,
Commentary on the Gospel of Matthew, 26, 27

[God] infuses life-giving power into the oblations and trans-mutes them into the virtue of His own flesh.

— Cyril of Alexandria,
Homilies on the Gospel of Luke, 22, 19

Against Apollinarius: "Refuse thou to allow that the body is by nature on par with the Godhead. Even though thou believe the body of the Christ to be real and bring it to the altar for transformation and fail to distinguish the nature of the body and of the Godhead we shall say to thee, 'If thou offer rightly and fail to distinguish rightly, thou sinnest; hold thy peace.' Distinguish what belongs naturally to us, and what is peculiar to the Word."

— Theodoret of Cyrus, A.D. 386–458,
Dialogues II; NPNF II, v. 3, p. 206

[Christ] took the bread and the cup, each in a similar fashion, and said: "This is My Body and this is My Blood." Not a fig-ure of His body nor a figure of His blood, as some persons of petrified mind are wont to rhapsodize, but in truth the Body and the Blood of Christ, seeing that His body is from the earth, and the bread and wine are likewise from the earth.

— Marcarius the Magnesian, A.D. 400,
Apocriticus, 3, 23; *FEF*, v. 3, 2166

When the Lord says: "Unless you shall have eaten the flesh of the Son of Man and shall have drunk His blood, you shall not have life in you," you ought to so communicate at the Sacred Table that you have no doubt whatever of the truth of the Body and the Blood of Christ. For that which is taken in the mouth is what is believed in faith; and in do those respond, "Amen," who argue against that which is received.

— Pope Leo I, A.D. 440–461,
Sermons; PL, 54, 91, 3; *FEF,* v. 3, 2214

As often as some infirmity overtakes a man, let him who is ill receive the Body and Blood of Christ; let him humbly and in faith ask the presbyters for blessed oil, to anoint his body, so that what was written may be fulfilled in him: "Is anyone among you sick? Let him bring in the presbyters, and let them pray over him, anointing him with oil."

— Caesarius of Arles, A.D. 470–542,
Sermons 13 [265], 3; *FEF,* v. 3, 2234

Afterword

As I stated in the Preface, the doctrine of the Eucharist is one of the most divisive of all doctrines between Catholics and Protestants. In fact, I would say that it is the ultimate dividing line. Why? Because of the consequences that follow from one's decision regarding the Eucharist. These consequences are spiritual life for the one whose decision is correct, and spiritual death for the one whose decision is incorrect. In other words, faith in the Eucharist is a question of heaven or hell.

Let me explain by presenting the question the way I have presented it to countless of Protestant friends. This method has never failed to engage the honest Protestant Christian who loves Jesus and wants to do His will. By God's grace, the way in which I have presented this question has resulted in many Protestants embracing the truth of the Eucharist. Unfortunately, it has also resulted in the termination of many friendships and associations. This has convinced me that the Catholic understanding of the Eucharist is indeed the dividing line between truth and error, between light and darkness, between Peter and Judas.

I explain to my Protestant friend that, in the Catholic Church, I worship what appears to be a piece of bread. Based on Scripture and 2,000 years of Christian tradition, I believe that in the Mass the bread becomes the body of Christ. If I am wrong, and the bread remains bread, then I am committing idolatry and risking eternal damnation for such a grave sin. However, if I am correct, then I am enjoying the most intimate union with Christ this side of heaven, and my Protestant friend is risking eternal damnation. Why? Because Jesus said, "Unless you eat the flesh of the Son of man and drink his blood, *you have no life in you*" (Jn 6:53). If Christ says we have "no life" in us, then we are spiritually dead. Thus, Jesus reveals that faith in the Eucharist is a question of salvation or damnation.[1]

If I am committing idolatry, then I tell my non-Catholic friend that he has a moral obligation to stop me and prove to me why I am wrong. As a Christian who loves me and desires my salvation, he cannot allow me to remain in my sin. He cannot stay "on the fence" while I continue my idolatrous worship. He must engage himself in this discussion by examining the Scriptures and what the early Christians believed. And he must share the fruits of his research with me and my fellow Catholics. As a matter of charity and justice, he cannot just walk away and leave me offending God, or he would be no friend at all. In fact, if he would walk away without engaging me, he would be condoning my idolatry and guilty of serious sin.

This question must provoke any honest non-Catholic Christian who loves his neighbor as himself to take a stand. This stand must be either to embrace the Catholic faith and receive the Bread of Life, or to reject it completely and base that rejection on the Scriptural, patristic, and historical witness — and especially the plain and simple words of Our Savior. This is why "just being a good Christian" is not enough to make it to heaven. Just as God requires faith in the Incarnation, He requires faith in the Eucharist — the extension of the Incarnation and the foundation of the New Covenant. I pose this challenge to my Protestant friends and conclude by asking them a question: "Will you also go away?" (Jn 6:67). Indeed, the doctrine of the Eucharist is where truth and error go their separate ways.

---

[1] I am not referring to those who are invincibly ignorant of their moral obligation to be Catholic and to have faith in the Eucharist. I am referring only to those who are culpable for their rejection of the Catholic Church and of the Eucharist. In either case, only God can judge the condition of these souls.

APPENDIX A

Miracles of the Eucharist

Throughout the history of the Roman Catholic Church, God has provided many miracles to further convict the world of the Church's teaching on the Real Presence of Christ in the Eucharist. Miracles in the lives of the saints are well-documented. During the reception of Holy Communion, the bodies of saints like Ignatius of Loyola (d. 1556), John of the Cross (d. 1591), and Alphonsus Liguori (d. 1787) would glow as they were enraptured in ecstasy. Clare of Assisi (d. 1253) and Teresa of Avila (d. 1594) would hear the voice of Jesus or the angels. Margaret Mary Alocoque (d. 1690) was given profound visions of Christ, as was Columba of Rieti (d. 1501) and Lawrence of Brindisi (d. 1619). Angela Merici (d. 1540), John of Cupertino (d. 1603), and Francis Solano (d. 1610) would levitate in the air.

Some saints would eat nothing but the Eucharist for many days and months, like Gerasimus (d. 475), Ita (d. 569), Catherine of Siena (d. 1380), Rita of Cascia (d. 1456), Catherine Fieschi of Genoa (d. 1510), and Mary Anne de Paredes (d. 1645). In fact, some saints survived on nothing but the bread of life for five, ten, and even twenty years! This is documented in the lives of Angela of Foligno (d. 1309), Lidwina (d. 1433), Nicholas of Flue (d. 1487), and Joseph of Cupertino (d. 1663). Many more incredible miracles have been written about in the lives of holy Catholic men and women.

Sometimes, God has intruded with miracles because of the doubt, indifference, or abuse people have demonstrated toward the Eucharist. On occasion, consecrated Hosts have turned to flesh, bled, levitated, and remained incorrupt. Through these supernatural interventions, God gives us more reason to have faith in His New Covenant and the awesome mystery of His love.

Chronicling the many miracles of the Eucharist is well beyond the scope of this book. It would be next to impossible to write about all of them. The purpose of this appendix is to give the reader a brief list of some of the miracles God has performed via the Eucharist — which, of course, is a miracle of its own. These accounts contain many more interesting facts that have been omitted.[1] I hope that this summary inspires the readers to a more intensive study of these miracles and deeper reverence of the "Sacrament of the Altar." Following is a list of some of the more well-known miracles of the Eucharist.

Lanciano, Italy (eighth century):

During the sacrifice of the Mass, the Host turned into flesh and the wine into five pellets of visible blood. In 1970, doctors of anatomy examined the flesh and blood pellets and documented the following: the flesh was striated muscular tissue of the myocardium (heart wall); the flesh and blood belonged to the same blood type, AB (the same blood type as that on the Shroud of Turin); and, the blood contained many common minerals and proteins. Today, the flesh and blood, still intact, are kept in a tabernacle in the Church of St. Francis in Lanciano and are open to the public for adoration.

Ferrara, Italy (1171):

During the Fraction Rite (the time in the Mass when the priest breaks the Host into two pieces), the Host gushed blood and

---

[1] For more information, I recommend the book *Eucharistic Miracles* (Tan Books and Publishers, Inc.) by Joan Carroll Cruz.

turned into flesh. Popes Eugene IV, Benedict XIV, and Pius IX have publicly recognized the miracle. In 1500, the church in which the miracle occurred was enlarged into a basilica. The basilica houses a vault which contains the holy blood and is seen and reverenced by the faithful to this day.

Augsburg, Germany (1194):

A Host became flesh and was visibly held together by stringy veins. After being transferred to the cathedral, the Host of flesh expanded in size, breaking the wax casing in which it was enclosed. The bishop ordered the Host to be enclosed in a crystal container and returned to the Church of the Holy Cross. Today, the blood-red Host remains in the same condition it has been in for over 800 years.

Alatri, Italy (1228):

A stolen Host turned to flesh. The miraculous Host was recovered and is kept in a chapel in the Cathedral of Alatri, where it is exhibited twice a year. It has remained in the same condition for almost 800 years.

Santarem, Portugal (c. 1230):

A stolen Host began to bleed profusely and emanate a blazing light. The Host was also miraculously encased in a crystal pyx. Today, the Host is enclosed in a monstrance and exhibits the presence of both dried and fresh blood at different times. These manifestations have been affirmed by medical physicians. St. Stephen's church has been renamed "The Church of the Holy Miracle." The bloody Host has endured in its state for over 700 years.

Florence, Italy (1230):

Some consecrated wine (the Precious Blood) was left in a chalice and turned into visible coagulated blood. After 775 years, the clump of blood looks the same today as it did in 1230, free from the influence of physical, chemical, or biological agents.

Daroca, Spain (1239):

Six consecrated Hosts were preserved between two corporals (linen cloths) during a battle between the Valencians and Saracens. During the battle, the Hosts turned into six blood stains. A church in the nearby town of Daroca was built in honor of the miracle and to house the corporals. Today, it is known as St. Mary's Collegiate Church. Visitors can go to the church and see the miraculous corporals on which the stains of Christ's blood are still clearly visible.

Olmütz, Czechoslovakia (Czech Republic) (1242):

Five consecrated Hosts were taken into a battle against the Tartars. After the Catholic soldiers defeated their enemies, the Hosts were returned to the church. It was then discovered that a shiny rosy color circle miraculously emanated from the Hosts. The miracle was witnessed by the entire congregation and all gave glory to God.

Bolsena-Orvieto, Italy (1263):

During the sacrifice of the Mass, blood began to spurt from the consecrated Host over the priest's hands and onto the corporal, altar, and floor. Pope Urban IV confirmed the miracle and enshrined the bloodstained corporal in the Cathedral of Orvieto, where it is still venerated today. In the Chapel of the Miracle, one can still see the stains of Christ's blood on the floor of the chapel.

Paris, France (1274):

A stolen Host began to levitate about the thief's head. When the priest who consecrated the Host arrived on the scene, the Host descended into the priest's hands. Many were present and witnessed the activity of the miraculous Host. The Host was returned to the church from which it was stolen and remained incorrupt until it disappeared during the French Revolution.

Slavonice, Czechoslovakia (Czech Republic) (1280):

A stolen Host suddenly appeared in the middle of a blazing fire, unaffected by the flames. When it was retrieved by the priest to be returned to the church, it miraculously appeared amidst the fire once again. A chapel was built on the spot of the fire but was destroyed by invaders in the fifteenth century. A new chapel called The Church of Christ's Holy Body was built on the same spot in 1476. To this day, Holy Mass is celebrated on the altar that is situated upon the stone heap where the miracle occurred.

Offida, Italy (1280):

A stolen Host turned into a piece of bloody flesh that stained a tablecloth and tile. The Host, tablecloth, and tile were then buried for seven years. When retrieved, the bloody Host and stained tile were uncontaminated. Today, the Sanctuary of the Miraculous Eucharist in Offida houses the reliquary containing the Host atop the main altar. The sanctuary also keeps the tablecloth and tile in a glass case. The blood smears on the tablecloth and tile are still visible.

Paris, France (1290):

A stolen Host that was stabbed with a knife violently spurted out blood from the cut marks, levitated in the air, and was unaffected by fire and boiling water. The miraculous Host was taken to the Church of St. Jean-en-Greve where it was adored with special services. A chapel was built on the site in which the miracle occurred and attracted many pilgrims until it was taken over by Lutherans in 1812.

Hasselt, Belgium (1317):

A Host began to bleed after it was touched by someone in mortal sin. The Host was enshrined at the church of the Cistercian nuns at Herkenrode, who were known for their holiness. At the service, as the priest placed the Host on the altar, everyone in the church saw a vision of Jesus crowned with thorns. Today, the Host is kept in the Church of St. Quentin in Hasselt. After nearly 700 years, the miraculous Host remains stained with blood and incorrupt.

Siena, Italy (1330):

A Host that was placed by a priest between pages of his breviary began to bleed and melt. One of the bloody pages is a relic in the Church of St. Augustine and has been venerated by Popes Boniface IX, Gregory XII, Sixtus IV, Innocent XIII, Clement XII, and Pius VII. In 1962, scientists confirmed the presence of coagulated human blood on the page. The scientists also discovered in the bloodstain the profile image of a man which has been captured by many photographs. Today, the relic is found in the Basilica-Sanctuary of St. Rita in Cascia, along with the incorrupt body of St. Rita and the bones of Blessed Simone Fidati.

Blanot, France (1331):

During Mass, a Host that fell out of a communicant's mouth and dropped on the linen cloth turned into a blood stain. After Mass, when the priest attempted to wash the stain, it became larger and darker. Diocesan officials later investigated the miracle, which was confirmed by Pope John XXII. Copies of the documents verifying the miracle are still kept in the City Hall of Blanot. Today, each year on Easter Monday, the relic of the bloody cloth is exposed in the church of Blanot.

Amsterdam, Netherlands (1345):

A sick man received Holy Communion and then vomited. His stomach contents were dumped into a lit fireplace. The next morning, the Host miraculously appeared intact among the burning coals. The bishop confirmed the miracle. A chapel was built on the site but was destroyed by fire about 100 years later. However, amid the ruins, the miraculous Host was found once again, completely intact.

Macerata, Italy (1356):

During the Fraction Rite, blood began to drip from the edges of the separated Host and onto the corporal. The bishop ordered a canonical examination and confirmed the miracle. Today, the blood stained corporal, clearly visible to the eye, is housed in a chapel in the Cathedral of Macerata and is honored during the octave of Corpus Christi.

Brussels, Belgium (1370):

Sixteen stolen Hosts were subjected to grave sacrilege at the hands of Jews in a synagogue in Belgium. When the Jews stabbed the Hosts, blood spurted forth from the stab wounds and the attackers were seized with terror. The bishop's office retrieved the Hosts, and they were taken to the Church of Notre Dame de la Chapelle and the Cathedral of St. Michael. The Cathedral contains various depictions of the miracle through sculptures, tapestries, and stained glass windows.

Middleburg-Louvain, Belgium (1374):

During Holy Communion, a Host that was received by a communicant in mortal sin turned to bleeding flesh. The blood dripped from the communicant's lips and stained the cloth on the altar railing. A few years later, the Host miraculously divided by itself. Today, half of the Host and bloodstained cloth is in the church of St. Jacques and half in Louvain where the flesh-colored Host and stained cloth are still visible. The miracle has been recognized by Popes Eugene IV, Alexander VII, Paul V, and Clement XIV.

Seefeld, Austria (1384):

During Mass, a Host began to bleed in the mouth of a man (a powerful knight) who made a sacrilegious communion. Further, as he received the Eucharist, the knight began to sink into the stone pavement. When he grabbed the altar to secure himself, his hands also sunk into the stone. The priest removed the Host and it was saturated with blood. The church, St. Oswald's, was enlarged in honor of the miracle. Today, the imprint of the knight's hands on the altar, the hollow in the floor, and the monstrance containing the miraculous Host have been made part of a special sanctuary in the church and are available for viewing.

Dijon, France (c. 1433):

A Host began to bleed after being treated sacrilegiously. The Host was adored in Rome for a time and then presented by Pope Eugene IV to Duke Philippe the Good of Burgundy. The Duke chose to enshrine the Host in la Sainte Chapelle (Holy Chapel) in Dijon. During the French Revolution, the Host was transferred to St. Michel's church but disappeared during this tumultuous period.

Turin, Italy (1453):

A stolen Host levitated in the air and gave off brilliant rays of light in front of the Church of San Silvestro. Scores of bystanders, including the bishop, witnessed the miracle. The bishop presented a chalice to the levitating Host while on his knees, and the Host descended into the chalice. The miraculous Host was transferred to the Cathedral of St. John the Baptist (wherein the Holy Shroud is also kept) and remained incorrupt for 131 years. Popes Pius II, Gregory XVI, Clement XIII, Benedict XIV, St. Pius X, and Pius XI have recognized the miracle. The Holy See ultimately ordered the Host to be consumed in thanksgiving to God.

Morrovalle, Italy (1560):

A Host remained perfectly intact after the Church of St. Francis, in which it was housed, burned to the ground. Even though the tabernacle in which the Host was kept along with the other sacred vessels was burned to ashes, the pure white Host was discovered lying upon a burned corporal. Pope Pius IX formally recognized the miracle. The Church of St. Francis was restored and is visited by many pilgrims to this day. It is speculated that the Host was stolen during the unrest of the nineteenth century, but the pyx in which the Host was preserved still exists.

Florence, Italy (1595):

Hosts which fell to the floor during a church fire united together from the heat but did not burn. After more than 400 years, the united body of Hosts remains unchanged and incorrupt. The Hosts can be seen in the Church of San Ambrogio, along with the chalice of the miracle of 1230 (the chalice that contains Christ's coagulated blood).

Alcala de Henares, Spain (1597):

Stolen Hosts were returned to the church, but the priest was not sure if they had been consecrated. The Hosts were preserved in the church's pantry and, after eleven years, remained white and incorrupt. The Hosts were then placed in a subterranean vault along with unconsecrated hosts to see if humidity would spoil them. After a few months, the unconsecrated hosts had withered, but the original Hosts remained incorrupt. The miraculous Hosts were eventually transferred to Holy Magistral Church and disappeared during the Spanish Civil War.

Faverney, France (1608):

A Host in a monstrance levitated in the air during a church fire. The Host and monstrance were unaffected by the fire while the altar, linens, vessels, and ornaments all burned to ashes. The levitation lasted thirty-three hours, the same number of years as Our Lord lived. During this time, the sacrifice of the Mass was offered in the presence of the levitating Host. Over fifty witnesses confirmed the miracle. The monstrance was destroyed during the French Revolution, but the miraculous Host was preserved and is kept in the Chapel of the Ostensorium in the Basilica of Faverney.

Siena, Italy (1730):

Stolen Hosts were discovered in an Offertory Box in the Church of St. Mary of Provenzano and retrieved. Having been retained for fifty years, the Hosts were found to be incorrupt. A scientific examination ten years later also found the Hosts to be without any sign of deterioration. The Hosts were placed in a box with unconsecrated hosts and sealed. After another sixty years, the box was opened and the unconsecrated hosts deteriorated while the divine Hosts remained fresh and unaltered. In 1914, Pope St. Pius X ordered a scientific investigation resulting in the same conclusion — the incorrupt Hosts defied the laws of nature. Popes St. Pius X, Benedict XV, Pius XI and Pius XII have recognized the miracle. Today, the miraculous Hosts can be seen in the Basilica of St. Francis in Siena.

Paterno, Italy (1772):

Stolen Hosts that were evidently buried in the ground sprang forth from the base of a tree and gathered into a ball of dazzling bright light. After a few moments, the levitating Hosts returned to the ground at the base of the tree. Witnesses of the miracle dug the miraculous Hosts up from the ground. Two nights later, in a nearby vicinity, flames and a glowing light moving up and down attracted more attention. A search was conducted beneath the area, and Hosts were found again. The Archdiocese of Naples maintains to this day records authenticating the miracle of the stolen Hosts.

Bordeaux, France (1822):

During adoration of the Blessed Sacrament, the Host disappeared and the accidents of Jesus Christ (head, chest, and arms) appeared in the monstrance instead. This miracle was witnessed by the celebrating priest and the congregation. The vision lasted for twenty minutes and the miracle was recognized by the Archbishop of Bordeaux and Popes Leo XII and Benedict XV. The monstrance is kept in the Ladies of Loreto house in Bordeaux.

Dubna, Poland (1867):

During adoration of the Blessed Sacrament, rays of light burst from the Host and Our Savior appeared in the monstrance. The vision endured throughout the service and was witnessed by many Catholics and non-Catholics alike. News of the miracle spread throughout Poland, in spite of efforts by the government to suppress it.

Stich, West Germany (1970):

During the Sacrifice of the Mass, blood spots suddenly appeared on the corporal next to the chalice. The spots were later examined by scientists and determined to be human blood. About a month later, the same priest celebrated Mass in the same chapel. Again, blood spots miraculously appeared on the corporal. Another examination confirmed that the spots were human blood.

The miracles have been authenticated by independent scientists and other witnesses. The corporals are kept in the shrine of Maria Rhein.

The Dogmatic Canons of the Council of Trent

The Canons on the Most Holy Sacrament of the Eucharist, Session XIII, Pope Julius III, October 11, 1551[1]

Canon 1. If anyone denies that in the sacrament of the most Holy Eucharist there are truly, really, and substantially contained the body and blood together with the soul and divinity of our Lord Jesus Christ, and therefore the whole Christ, but shall say that He is in it as by a sign, or figure, or force: let him be anathema.[2]

Canon 2. If anyone says that in the sacred and holy sacrament of the Eucharist there remains the substance of bread and wine together with the body and blood of our Lord Jesus Christ, and denies that wonderful and singular conversion of the whole substance of the bread into the body, and of the entire substance of the wine into the blood, the species of bread and wine only remaining, a change which the Catholic Church most fittingly calls transubstantiation: let him be anathema.

Canon 3. If anyone denies that the whole Christ is contained in the venerable sacrament of the Eucharist under each species and under every part of each species, when the separation has been made: let him be anathema.

---

[1] *Enchiridion Symbolorum*, Henry Denzinger (1957), 883-893.

[2] *Anathema* is a Greek word that means to be "set apart," that is, excommunicated or accursed.

Canon 4. If anyone says that after the completion of the consecration that the body and blood of our Lord Jesus Christ is not in the marvelous sacrament of the Eucharist, but only in use, while it is taken, not however before or after, and that in the hosts or consecrated particles, which are reserved or remain after communion, the true body of the Lord does not remain: let him be anathema.

Canon 5. If anyone says that the special fruit of the most Holy Eucharist is the remission of sins, or that from it no other fruits are produced: let him be anathema.

Canon 6. If anyone says that in the holy sacrament of the Eucharist, the only-begotten Son of God is not to be adored even outwardly with the worship of latria (the act of adoration), and therefore not to be venerated with a special festive celebration, nor to be borne about in procession according to the praiseworthy and universal rite and custom of the holy Church, or is not to be set before the people publicly to be adored, and that the adorers of it are idolaters: let him be anathema.

Canon 7. If anyone says that it is not lawful that the Holy Eucharist be reserved in a sacred place, but must necessarily be distributed immediately after consecration among those present; or that it is not permitted to bring it to the sick with honor: let him be anathema.

Canon 8. If anyone says that Christ received in the Eucharist is received only spiritually, and not also sacramentally and in reality: let him be anathema.

Canon 9. If anyone denies that all and each of the faithful of Christ of both sexes, when they have reached the years of discretion, are bound every year to communicate at least at Easter according to the precept of holy mother Church: let him be anathema.

Canon 10. If anyone says that it is not lawful for a priest celebrating to communicate himself: let him be anathema.

Canon 11. If anyone says that faith alone is sufficient preparation for receiving the sacrament of the most Holy Eucharist: let him be anathema. And that so great a sacrament may not be unworthily received, and therefore unto death and condemnation, this holy council ordains and declares that sacramental confession must necessarily be made beforehand by those whose conscience is burdened by mortal sin, however contrite they may consider themselves. If anyone moreover teaches the contrary or preaches or obstinately asserts, or even publicly by disputation shall presume to defend the contrary, by that itself he is excommunicated.

THE CANONS ON THE SACRIFICE OF THE MASS, SESSION XXII, POPE PIUS IV, SEPTEMBER 17, 1562[3]

Canon 1. If anyone says that in the Mass a true and proper sacrifice is not offered to God or that the offering consists merely in the fact that Christ is given to us to eat, *anathema sit.*

Canon 2. If anyone says that by the words, 'Do this as a memorial of me' Christ did not establish the apostles as priests or that he did not order that they and other priests should offer his body and blood, *anathema sit.*

Canon 3. If anyone says that the sacrifice of the Mass is merely an offering of praise and thanksgiving, or that it is a simple commemoration of the sacrifice accomplished on the cross, but not a propitiatory sacrifice, or that it benefits only those who communicate; and that it should not be offered for the living and the dead, for sins, punishments, satisfaction, and other necessities, *anathema sit.*

---

[3] *The Christian Faith: Doctrinal Documents*, ed. Jacques Dupuis, 1555-1563.

Canon 4. If anyone says that the sacrifice of the Mass constitutes a blasphemy against the most holy sacrifice which Christ accomplished on the cross, or that it detracts from that sacrifice, *anathema sit.*

Canon 5. If anyone says that it is an imposture to celebrate Masses in honor of the saints and in order to obtain their intercession with God as the Church intends, *anathema sit.*

Canon 6. If anyone says that the Canon of the Mass contains errors and therefore should be abolished, *anathema sit.*

Canon 7. If anyone says that the ceremonies, vestments, and external signs which the Catholic Church uses in the celebration of Masses, are incentives to impiety rather than works of piety, *anathema sit.*

Canon 8. If anyone says that Masses in which the priest alone communicates sacramentally, are illicit and therefore should be abolished, *anathema sit.*

Canon 9. If anyone says that the rite of the Roman Church prescribing that part of the Canon and the words of consecration to be pronounced in a low tone is to be condemned; or that Mass should be celebrated only in the vernacular; or that water should not be mixed with the wine to be offered in the chalice because this would be contrary to Christ's institution, *anathema sit.*

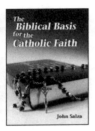